MAK[...]
TR[...]

Few can claim to have precipitated fundamental change in the jewellery business, but Greg Valerio is one of those who can. As a standard bearer for the principle that ethically sourced jewellery can serve as agent for sustainable economic and social development, he has helped transform the way in which we regard ourselves and the products we produce and sell.

Gaetano Cavalieri – President of The World Jewellery Confederation

This is a fantastic story about how one man wouldn't take no for an answer, and has such a powerful vision of creating change in the gold sector.

Harriet Lamb CBE – CEO of Fairtrade International

Making Trouble is a thrilling expose of the jewellery industry from one of its inside-men. Greg Valerio exorcises the demons of capitalism and takes the bull by the horns. He unveils the ugliness of the beauty business, and exposes the dark side of the dazzle. His truth has a sting, but he also has an unflinching, contagious hope that a better world is possible. And he invites you to stir up trouble with him by making injustice less and less fashionable.

Shane Claiborne – Activist and founding member of The Simple Way, Philadelphia

MAKING
FIGHTING FOR FAIR TRADE JEWELLERY
TROUBLE

GREG VALERIO

LION

Published by Lion Books
an imprint of
Lion Hudson plc
Wilkinson House, Jordan Hill Road,
Oxford OX2 8DR, England
www.lionhudson.com/lion

ISBN 978 0 7459 5603 9
e-ISBN 978 0 7459 5754 8

First edition 2013

Acknowledgments

Unless otherwise stated, epigraphs are by Greg Valerio.
pp. 75–76: Poem "Que Pasa Condoto" is © Greg Valerio.

Scripture quotations are from The New Revised Standard Version of the Bible copyright © 1989 by the Division of Christian Education of the National Council of Churches in the USA. Used by permission. All Rights Reserved.

A catalogue record for this book is available from the British Library

Printed and bound in the UK, August 2013, LH26

Dedication

There are many people I should thank and who have played a part in shaping my story to date.

The people at ARM and Fairtrade for their unswerving dedication to the creation of Fairtrade gold. All those who worked for CRED over the years, who without complaining proved that full traceability in jewellery from mine to retail is possible. For Micha Jazz (Mike Morris in our story) who saw the potential in a young man when no one else did, and who remains a source of wisdom to me all these years later.

My mum and dad for putting up with me in my wayward teenage years. I caused them untold grief and parental anxiety and I hope they see it turned out all right in the end.

And of course to Ruth, my wife, and my two daughters, Mali-Grace and Jemba-May, who let me travel to the remotest parts of the world, were constant in their belief of success, and remain a harbour of peace, tranquillity, and endless fun. I love you to the stars and back.

CONTENTS

— FOREWORD
9

— CHAPTER ONE
12

— CHAPTER TWO
28

— CHAPTER THREE
45

— CHAPTER FOUR
60

— CHAPTER FIVE
77

— CHAPTER SIX
90

— CHAPTER SEVEN
106

— CHAPTER EIGHT
124

— CHAPTER NINE
138

— CHAPTER TEN
155

— CHAPTER ELEVEN
170

— EPILOGUE
187

— GLOSSARY
198

— END NOTE TO CONSUMERS
200

— NOTES
203

FOREWORD

It is not easy combining campaigning, running a business, having a family, and being cursed with a conscience that won't allow you to turn a blind eye to the obvious stupidity that so often stares us in the face.

Greg Valerio has battled through the whole process indomitably from the jungles of Colombia and the metal workshops of Jaipur to the emerging ruby veins newly exposed by the retreating ice sheet in Greenland. He is the pioneer of fair trade jewellery and a true hero.

Campaigning is all about creating the alternative, offering a solution. When I first discovered the toxic impact that pesticides used in the fashion industry's cotton supply chain was having on the farmers and the workers in the cotton fields, I would go to trade fairs asking for organic cotton, only to be treated to their looks of blank incredulity and vacant expressions of mild amusement at my eccentricity. "Why should we do it, since you are the only one asking for it?" they said, which was pretty shocking. The industry was ignorant but even when it knew, it didn't care.

Pesticides are a curse; just look at what neonicotinoids are doing to our precious bees and pollinators.

In conventional agriculture, 10,000 people die every year from accidental pesticide poisoning, and a further million are hospitalized. Pesticides create long-term contamination of the aquifer and microbiological death in soil, leading to desertification.

In one area of India there have been 250,000 suicides due to pesticide debt. Yet there is an alternative: farmers can increase their profits by between 50 to 500 per cent by farming organically with specific crop rotation, allowing them to feed and clothe their families, educate their children, and afford health care, which isn't the case for most cotton farmers right now.

We have to care. A civilization falls apart when its citizens stop caring about their fellow men. It's why we are here. There is a mistranslation in Genesis 1 – "dominion" should read "partnership", "guardianship", "control". We are responsible for looking after life on earth and the planet we have been given.

The kind of world we have allowed to happen is a mess we are going to leave our children. I for one don't want to live in a world that ignores the consequences of its consumptive demands, or a political landscape where large industries and government that they own are allowed to wreak havoc with our human rights, democracy, and the future of our planet.

"How We Consume Decides the Future of the Planet" says a T-shirt I made for CRED. It's true. Voting with our wallets is the most immediate democratic impact the average citizen has. Informed consumers, asking for sustainable product and not buying products because they were concerned about where they came from or how they were made, have driven the clothing industry to improve its supply chain in some cases. Incredibly, by itself it would have done nothing.

It's hard, changing things. You need to be determined, persevering, and have a tireless compassion for humanity, optimism, and a firm belief that we can make a better world.

Greg has been extraordinarily dogged in his quest for the ugly truth that is behind the global jewellery business. The status quo is untenable. Consumers don't want a wedding ring that has been responsible for 3 tonnes of persistent toxic waste (mercury, cyanide) that kills all the fish down stream and poisons the local drinking water that has paid for AK47s and funded the brutalization of women and children in the Congo.

It might just be that the road to securing fair trade gold is a step toward saving our future. Sustainable supply chains are the only long-term, viable economic development model. But what is for sure is that it has informed consumers and shown an entire industry what is wrong with the rest of the luxury jewellery business.

Consumers reading this book, and their concerns being reflected in their buying patterns, are going to change the face of jewellery sourcing forever.

Well done, Greg.

Katharine Hamnett, CBE
Fashion designer and campaigner

CHAPTER ONE

Valerio, you're a natural-born troublemaker.

"Oh no!"

There was a shout of utter despair from the next room. I rushed in to see my wife, Ruth, standing next to an ironing board, iron in hand, her blue silk dress laid out on the board. She had a look of complete anguish on her face.

"What's wrong?" I asked.

"I've burned a hole into my dress for tonight's ceremony."

I guessed this was not the best moment to see the funny side of life.

Ruth had burned an iron-shaped hole the size of the palm of her hand through the dress at the top of her left thigh. We tried desperately to work out how, in the next ten minutes, we could resolve the problem. After a few frantic phone calls to anyone we thought would be able to help, we came to the realization that we did not know many people in Willesden, north London. Ruth would have to attend the ceremony in the offending dress and wander around with her left hand strategically placed over the hole. Thankfully, she was beginning to see the amusing side of it.

As we arrived at the Natural History Museum, I became increasingly aware of what a big event this really was. The Observer Ethical Awards ceremony recognizes the myriad of British ethical and campaign talent in the UK. I was up for Campaigner of the Year, against the amazing Avaaz network, whose online campaigning could muster millions of global signatures on a particular issue in a matter of hours, and the indomitable Greenpeace, whose direct action campaigning has been the inspiration of generations as they have fought for a more sustainable planet.

My work in securing certified fair trade gold from the hands of small-scale miners and to promote full transparency and traceability throughout the jewellery supply chain had come to the attention of Lucy Siegle, the BBC ethical broadcaster and Guardian columnist, whose job it was to host the annual awards.

As we arrived I was greeted by the CRED Jewellery staff and the Fairtrade Foundation people who I had worked with so closely to secure fair trade gold, and also Ameriko Mosquera, the Oro Verdé ecological gold miner from Chocó, Colombia, whom I had first met in 2004. It was this meeting that had created the spark that would eventually lead to the creation of fair trade gold, and it was fitting that he was with us for the evening.

It was exciting. Lots of people I had never met before came and congratulated me on the "great work". Ameriko was sipping his champagne and drinking in the museum's wonderful architecture. It was a far cry from the jungles of Colombia.

Lucy introduced Livia Firth, actor Colin Firth's wife, whose job it was to announce the winner of Campaigner of the Year award. I was delighted that I had been nominated. I did not expect to win; if I had been on the award committee, I would have voted for Avaaz. Their work reached far more people than fair trade gold had. But when Livia Firth said, "To win this category you need to be able to break a few balls along the way," I knew I had won.

My first reaction was to find Ameriko. Here was the man who stood in the muddy streams of Chocó with his family, and washed out the gold that supported them. This was the man who did not use mercury to process the gold, as so many thousands of small-scale miners around the world did. This was the man who replanted the forest as he went. To me, he represented the 100 million small-scale miners from around the world whose poverty and suffering had been ignored. He and others like him had inspired me; it was for men like Ameriko that I had campaigned so hard in the jewellery industry for their existence to be recognized.

Receiving the award, it felt as if I had come to the end of this particular part of my journey in jewellery. Fairtrade gold proved that making jewellery did not have to exploit people, or damage the environment. It proved that in creating a piece of jewellery, you could ensure that the miners who are linked to the gold that you use were getting a better deal for their hard work.

"Valerio, you're a natural-born troublemaker. Just make sure you make trouble for the right reasons." These were the parting words of my head of year, the day he officially expelled me from school. He was a softly spoken man, and I liked him. He treated me fairly and like a human being, which was a refreshing break from the monotonous middle-management expectations being set by a school that expected unquestioned conformity to a set of social norms more akin to Edwardian Britain than to the angst and disaffection fermenting in the early 1980s.

School, to me, was a farce, with its pressure to qualify with straight As, sit the Oxbridge exam, or end up working for IBM. This mantra was continually preached in classrooms and assemblies, yet how could I take this seriously when one of the female teachers seduced my classmates, and another one sold some of the best dope in the district? My disaffection with the school was reciprocated, because the senior staff did not like me very much either. They expressed their displeasure at wayward behaviour with the cane before it was outlawed.

Toward the end of my time at school, my attendance was almost non-existent. So when my head of year informed me, after a week's solitary confinement in his office (probably for getting caught smoking again), that he had spoken to my parents and that all parties agreed there was no point in me coming back, I was absolutely delighted. Screw the exams, screw the teachers, and screw it all. I had no idea what I would do, but I knew where I did not want to be. I did learn one vital lesson at school, though: "Always question everything. Always question authority, and take nothing they say for granted."

In truth, my school years were doomed even before I began, as I was being sexually abused by one of my scout leaders. This act of violence against my innocence would prove devastating. The early exuberance and ambition of my childhood potential disappeared into a hole of emotional turbulence and darkness. Confusion reigned, alongside the endless internal self-obsessing questions: Why did it happen? Why did I let it happen? Was it my fault? It created a surly rebelliousness that, coupled with my need to survive the trauma, meant I went from being a grade-A student to someone whose sole objective in life was to survive and try to make sense of the injustice. This was my first introduction to injustice, and the ensuing sense of powerlessness and exploitation at the hands of authority gave me a natural affinity with those who seemed to be suffering in a similar way.

This abuse of power caused a cascade of questions for me and stripped bare the pretences of all those who claimed to have authority. Being a teenager in the 1980s was not easy for me. Not only did school prove challenging, I found the stark social unrest in Britain deeply unsettling. I watched the television coverage of the rioting that broke out regularly across the urban centres of Britain, and the ideological-driven violence of the miners' strike, where the police ran pitched battles with the miners. The apparently cynical dismantling of mining communities by the Thatcher government made me cry at the suffering and futility of the entire situation.

The Cold War rhetoric of impending nuclear disaster provided a constant background noise, together with rising unemployment and general increasing social discontent, which was in turn rooted in disillusionment with the Establishment and a lack of opportunity for young people. I found no comfort in the world and felt completely out of place.

This led me to explore spirituality. Perhaps in a more esoteric world I would find the missing ingredient that could make sense of the social nihilism and hopelessness sweeping across the country I lived in. The external world around me seemed to be in total confusion, so maybe the internal world of spirituality could offer me a peace and purpose that the social and political world could not. My experimentation was more than just a passing fad. I was genuinely interested. I looked into spiritualism, Hinduism and Buddhism, neopaganism, and what was called the New Age movement.

Like most teenagers, I had rejected the church as socially irrelevant. I considered it a monolith to the past and responsible for propping up a world I felt I did not belong to. But I did not subscribe to the popular notion that "God is dead"; I had always found that idea ridiculous and intellectually unsupportable. I could not discount the existence of God purely on the basis of the church's social irrelevance or the scientifically reasoned argument rooted in a theory of evolution. To my mind, this was a very unreasonable position to hold. I would always argue with one of the science teachers, who was a militant evangelical atheist, that his position was untenable. He could not prove or disprove the existence of God; he could only hold an opinion like the rest of us. He was also a particularly miserable, cynical, and mean-spirited man. If this is what atheism produced, I wanted nothing to do with it. I think I probably got more detentions in physics than any other lesson.

Leaving school with no qualifications doesn't leave you with many options apart from going into the theatre. Now here was something I felt I could do. I loved reading, especially Shakespeare, was never short of an opinion on a subject (however ill-informed I may have been), and was pretty good with my mouth. I did a season at the Chichester Festival Theatre as stage crew and really enjoyed myself. Working on the pantomime Babes in the Wood opened up a door of potential opportunity. That season I got the chance to work with Spike Milligan, whose comic genius was matched only by the intensity of his melancholy.

I would be an actor. What fun. I would get the chance to meet talented, erudite people, and party most nights with subsidized alcohol and drugs. Bill Snape, the student coordinator from the Guildhall School of Music & Drama in London, used to do the pantomime circuit every year and became a good friend. He was the largest, most raucous, crude, foul-mouthed, screaming queen of a man I had ever met. Later to die of an HIV-related illness, Snape, alongside my girlfriend of the time, Vanya, encouraged me to start auditioning for drama school. All roads lead to London when it comes to the theatre, so I packed up my bags and moved to The Smoke at seventeen.

London in 1985 was a city in turmoil. I moved in with Vanya and her mum, who lived in Chiswick, and began walking Shaftesbury Lane, knocking on the backstage doors of all the theatres asking for work. After weeks of being fobbed off with the mantra "come back next week", I finally got a job at the Duke of York's on St Martin's Lane, working front of house. Seven shifts, including two matinees a week, every other weekend off, and £60 take-home a week, which was not enough to live on.

I subsidized my income by collecting money from public phone boxes through an ingenious use of a playing card inserted into the returned coin slot, modelling for a portrait painter, and earning tips from rich female theatregoers. I learned a trick from a colleague on the downstairs Stalls Bar. I would spot the perfume that women were wearing. It would break the ice, and often led to a fiver being left under the half-drunk champagne bottle. All this gave me an extra £15 to £20 a week, and lots of free champagne.

Working in the theatre meant working nights, in the London of the neon lights, the seedy backstreets, the homeless haunts under Waterloo Bridge, the Soho street girls, pimps, rich partygoers, and the aggressive gay cruisers looking for a quick pick-up. Every week I would find myself being propositioned. Some would offer a fiver, others would offer hundreds and, on one occasion, even £5,000 to fulfil their particular fantasy. I learned very quickly how to fend off the continual harassment with a well-constructed sentence that included the use of the F-word and a mention of my girlfriend. The widening social inequality with "yuppies" and bankers flaunting their wealth in the faces of the poor every day made me angry and jealous at the same time.

There were two types of theatregoer – those who loved theatre, and those who used it as a way to show off their money and success by treating others as skivvies. I was fortunate I had a job, but despite everything looking OK on the surface, underneath London was also turning out to be a lonely city, a bewildering environment for a seventeen-year-old to be wandering around in.

My daily routine would generally be to get up at midday, catch the tube from Turnham Green to Leicester Square, read for a few hours and then hit work at four o'clock. Weekends, when not working, I would go back to Chichester to see old friends who by all accounts did not seem to be doing any better than me. I was not making huge progress on the auditions, either. I applied to all the major London acting schools and they all said no. I was too young and just not good enough.

That summer, Vanya and I went to France for a holiday, and ended up sleeping rough in the Jardins des Tuileries, Paris. I got serious food poisoning, and spent the rest of the summer in Fréjus at my Aunt Jill's caravan with chronic haemorrhoids. When we got back, Vanya and I decided to give our relationship a rest. I moved out, relocated to Wood Green, and then promptly got thrown out by my landlord. I was homeless.

After a cold October of sleeping rough in Chiswick House gardens under the A4 flyover, I found a room in West Hampstead close to Abbey Road. It was only slightly better than being homeless, as the other rooms off the dark, damp, and dingy corridor were full of smack addicts. London was not working out as planned. Rather than climbing the greasy pole of fame and fortune, I was becoming another one of those naive victims who thought the streets of London were paved with gold. I had believed the flattery of others who were encouraging me to pursue a career in the theatre, when I was far too young and inexperienced to succeed there.

I was slowly being consumed by the relentless soul-destroying monotony of living on the breadline in a country of no opportunity. I was beginning to think the whole thing was a dead end.

Becoming a Christian was not something I was looking for, and would turn out to be the watershed in my relationship with London. Vanya's mother, actress Anna Cropper, had flown to India to film the Jewel in the Crown TV series. Vanya was travelling with her, and they asked if I would look after their Chiswick house for the six weeks. I agreed. It was better than a smack-infested corridor in West Hampstead.

On one of my afternoon journeys to the West End for work, I was sitting on a park bench outside Turnham Green tube station reading Jude the Obscure. It was a late summer afternoon, the sun was out, and London was busy as usual. In fact, everything was as it should be.

The only way I can describe what happened next was I had some form of waking vision of the person of Jesus. I instantly knew who it was, and the voice that spoke to me had a clarity that transcended explanation. "I want you to follow me. I have a job for you to do." Accompanying the voice was an overwhelming sense of peace and light. It was if the very core of my soul had been washed with fire, and I felt elated beyond words. Everything around me changed for what seemed like an eternity, but I am sure was only moments. I seemed to see the world as it truly was, rather than as it pretended to be. Colours became true, as though they were taking off the mask that hid their real identity, the noises around me became the music of a symphony, and, most importantly, I began to see myself as I truly was. It was not an encounter born of my emotional vulnerability in the face of my social loneliness: it was an affirmation that I was loved.

To this day, I have never been able to adequately find words to describe that moment. All I knew was I had met the person of Jesus Christ, that I was truly known and loved by him, and that I had come home.

As the melee of Chiswick began to overtake my encounter, there was no question or confusion in my mind. I knew what had happened, who I had met, what had been said to me. I got up, jumped on the tube, and went to work as normal. For weeks I told no one what had happened, as I could not find the words to describe the experience without the fear of sounding like a raving lunatic.

Eventually I decided to visit a guy I knew who was a Christian. I had to get some validation of what had happened. Maybe I was losing all touch with reality. Roger Ellis had been leading a local independent church in Chichester called Revelation since the early 1980s. Despite having appalling taste in music (he was a headbanger who listened to Scorpions, Rush, and other pretentious rock bands, and wore trousers that were just too tight for decency), he was one of the few men I had met who seemed to practice what they preached, so I considered him to have integrity. He told me my experience had been a genuine encounter with Jesus, and apparently this happened to thousands of people all over the world every day. Phew, I was not mad.

Back at work, as I was setting up the Stalls Bar for that evening's show, I was on the receiving end of an unsolicited tirade of abuse from one of my colleagues about the bigotry of "born-again Christians". As I had not told him or anyone else what had happened to me, this was all the more puzzling. Was I now one of those bigots? Was I one of those "born-again people?" I was confused; I did not have any answers. I decided at that point it was time to leave. I handed in my notice, moved back to Chichester, joined the church that Roger led, and got a job as a kitchen porter.

For the next couple of years, I lived in a holding pattern. It was during this time that I met Ruth, who eventually was to become my wife. She was doing her A levels at Haileybury boarding school in Hertfordshire and would come down to stay at her sister's place during half terms and holidays. In many ways she was my antithesis, in regards to education and outlook. She would go on to Cambridge University to read Theology and then do an MA at the London School of Theology. Ruth was the perfect foil to my turbulence, my continued disaffection, and confusion with my place in the world.

My initial euphoria surrounding becoming a Christian was wearing off, and the normal realities of life, earning a living, the day-to-day grind were beginning to eat away at my soul. I remember praying at the time, "Is this all there is?"

Mike Morris was one of the leaders of the church I was at, and he asked me if I would consider working in schools, doing Development Education. Clearly the man was mad. Did he not know I had no qualifications? However, Mike was a veteran campaigner, unfazed by tough assignments. He had lived in, and supported, the coal mining communities that were dismantled by Mrs Thatcher, was a member of the ANC and got involved in the struggle against apartheid, was active in smuggling Russian dissidents out of the USSR, and campaigned on behalf of the Vietnamese boat people who were being interned in refugee camps by the British authorities in Hong Kong.

He saw something in me that I, as a self-absorbed young man, could not. Mike had been talking to Christian Aid about them releasing some funding to develop a programme of education work on human rights and environmental justice issues across the south coast. He explained it would mean going in and taking lessons on a range of subjects related to international justice and the plight of the poor. He gave me a few books to read and left me to consider his proposal.[1]

Boredom got the better of me and I said yes. I liked what I had read and got very fired up about the state of the world's poor, and the fact that the situation could be resolved with the political will of the global community. I was reminded of Live Aid in 1985 and how moved I had been by the call to action in the face of such overwhelming tragedy, and the goodwill of ordinary people to meet the needs of the dying. Mike's offer gave me a way of finding a fresh purpose. I confess I had a huge internal prejudice to overcome as the idea of going into those sweaty, stale, hormone-infested institutions called schools filled me with dread. But it seemed a better option than being a kitchen porter.

The training the church put me through was rigorous. The law in the UK is very clear: you cannot proselytize in schools as pupils are a captive audience, so going there as a local church and Christian Aid representative meant I had to be extra diligent. Eventually, after many months of reading, preparing lesson plans and mock presentations, and struggling with feelings of unworthiness, I put together a small pack on the material I felt I could cover, how it related to the National Curriculum, and posted it to all the secondary schools on the south coast of England between Southampton and Brighton.

Then I sat back and waited.

Within days I had my first reply. My old school invited me in to take an assembly and a lesson on the Universal Declaration of Human Rights. As I walked into my old form room as a guest speaker and was introduced to the class as an old boy, the palpable shiver of irony swept through me as my former tutor gave way to me to address the class. Perhaps I really could do this.

Over the next few years, the Development Education programme grew very quickly. Very soon I was seeing thousands of pupils in lessons, assemblies, and day conferences right across the south of England. It caught me a little by surprise. I found the best form of learning is when you do it, so for pupils to really understand the issue, they had to get involved. So I got them campaigning on different issues, such as the cancellation of Third World debt, promoting Fairtrade products in their schools, writing letters about human rights cases promoted by Amnesty International, and boycotting Nestlé products over their unethical marketing of breast milk substitutes to mothers in Africa and Asia. We also supported any campaigns being run by our principal funder, Christian Aid.

But I felt a little fraudulent. I was delivering education on important international issues and the furthest I had travelled in my life was between Canada, where I was born, and the UK, to where my family had moved in 1976. That hardly represented exposure to the coalface of hard-core poverty. How could I represent the poorest of the poor if I had never sat down and listened to their stories? The closest I had come to poverty was being homeless in London, which was nothing compared to poverty in Africa. I explained all this to Mike Morris and he arranged for me to go on a summer trip to Tanzania with a well-respected Christian Non-governmental Organization (NGO).

The seven-week trip to live and work alongside local people in the rural south of Tanzania sounded ideal. I would be exposed to the daily poverty of ordinary Tanzanians, I could listen to their stories, their hopes and fears, and learn from them. I went with a group of six other individuals, all university students from different parts of the country. It turned out to be a seminal seven weeks.

Our basic job was brick-making for an extension to a school. Every day we would mix cement, dump it into the brick machine, turn out bricks, and lay them out in the sun to dry. After the initial week of excitement of new sights, sounds, smells, cuisine, using long-drop toilets, bucket showers, avoiding cobras, and endless meals of aubergine, the monotony and isolation began to set in. I learned to appreciate that poverty is not just about a lack of money, it is also about the lack of opportunities and the continual isolation of the soul from fulfilling the dreams we are all born with.

One conversation I had with a rural trainee pastor from a church brought home to me how thin the line between life and death really was. This pastor had bilharzia, a disease caused by a water-borne parasite that can kill you, over time, if not treated. As you weaken through the illness, you cannot work; if you cannot work, you cannot earn money to buy food; if you cannot eat, you weaken, and so the vicious cycle continues. This man had a wife and three children to feed. So what little money he did earn through subsistence farming he gave to his wife to feed his children. I asked him what the cure was. I was told a simple course of drugs would kill the parasite, but he could not afford to buy the treatment and feed his family at the same time. He was slowly dying so his children might live. When I enquired how much the course of treatment would be for him, I was informed about £5.

That evening our team discussed this man's situation. To me it was obvious what I should do. I had £5 in my wallet; I could just pay for the treatment. I was told this might not be culturally sensitive, as he was an elder. And if I did it for one person, I might have to do it for everyone.

"**** that!" I exclaimed. "What's culturally sensitive about dying and leaving your kids without a father?"

I gave the guy the money for his treatment; he was very grateful, we did not upset anyone in the process, and he got better.

After about the fourth week of making endless bricks (denying locals employment so the project could host white people from the donor organization), and eating endless aubergines with rice, cabin fever finally got the better of me. I negotiated a week off from the project to travel to Arusha in the north of the country, and booked a ticket with the Comfort Bus Company.

I learned right there about the deception of aspirational statements. The lady sitting next to me was five times my width, took up most of my seat as well as her seat, seemed to think eating my food was far more pleasurable than eating her own, and was accompanied by a flock of chickens that shat everywhere. I was enjoying public transport, African-style. As we bumped our way through the country, I breathed in the vast expanse of the Tanzanian horizon.

Arriving in Arusha, I found a cheap guesthouse and set about exploring the dusty streets and market stalls, drinking in the ebb and flow of daily life. A few hours into my bewildering yet enchanting meanderings around the city, a man tugged my arm gently and asked if I would like to see his batiks. Nothing new in that request; I was getting that question every ten minutes from the hustlers on every street corner. I was just about to deliver my stock response of "No, not really" when I caught his eye and saw the guy was genuinely not trying to hustle me. His gentleness was tangible and his voice was soft with no aggression.

Robert Mollel took me to his studio about half a mile out of the centre of town. The man was a genius. His canvasses were huge, abstract Picassoesque pieces, picturing traditional mystical landscapes and village scenes from the life of east Africa. His studio was scattered with all kinds of symbols of his Maasai heritage.

In one corner sat a small shield, bow and arrow, and a strange-looking handheld gourd with spikes sticking out. I was intrigued by the gourd and asked Robert what this was for. He explained that when he went hunting lions he used the shield, bow and arrow, and gourd as his weapons. He went on to elaborate. If you did not kill the lion with the bow and arrow, you used the spiked gourd.

"How do you kill a lion with that?" I exclaimed.

"You wait till the lion is almost upon you and, as it opens its mouth, you thrust the gourd into the mouth and twist."

Robert told the story in a very matter-of-fact way, with no embellishments. This was clearly something he had done on numerous occasions. He then moved on to asking me if I wanted to go on a lion hunt with him. I said no, as I would not have the time, but thanked him for his offer. Hunting lions was slightly outside of my skill set.

Robert was a Maasai man educated in the West, highly articulate, and a genuine artist. His story challenged me. Here was a man displaced from the Ngorongoro crater by his government to facilitate International Monetary Fund-backed economic structural adjustment policies (SAPs).[2] These policies were imposed on poorer countries such as Tanzania as a precondition to them being able to borrow on the international markets. The impact these SAPs had on developing countries was considerable. Food prices rose, and the country was forced to privatize its services, such as water and electricity, which meant increased prices. People like Robert and his family were forced to leave their ancestral lands so these could be turned into a national wildlife park that would attract tourists, so the country as a whole could earn more foreign currency.

SAPs created misery for millions of poor people across Africa. Roberts's family had to move to Arusha and he now earned his living from art. Having lost his traditional Maasai way of life, he was struggling to survive because he could not compete with the cheap tourist batiks sold by other locals.

I was deeply moved by his story. Here was a living example of an abuse of power on a grand scale, in which SAPs were having a negative impact on the ancestral livelihoods of ordinary people. Robert was not looking for charity, he was asking for a fair exchange for his artwork. Over the next few days we got to know each other quite well. When it was time for me to leave, he helped me to negotiate a genuinely comfortable bus ride back to Iringa, and I said goodbye with two of his batiks safely rolled up in my case.

I was now coming toward the end of my time in Tanzania. Each night, after everyone had gone to sleep, I would sit out on the steps of our little brick dormitory and allow the African stars to smile on me. The deep silence that is an African night was the perfect environment in which to reflect on what I had experienced. I had met the poverty I had read and taught about, and witnessed the fragility of life and the political stupidity that allowed such injustice to occur.

I also had big questions about the effectiveness of development money. I had spent six weeks making bricks in Tanzania with six other people. These were jobs that we had denied local people. The community, who benefited from the money the NGO granted them, felt obliged to give us this work, rather than employ local people. In some ways I had become a development tourist, with the NGO taking my money for the privilege of exposing me to extreme poverty.

It was a tough circle to square off. On the one hand I had gained invaluable experience of the power imbalances between rich and poor. On the other, I was deeply uncomfortable with the way I had to get this exposure. Yet I had also witnessed the intense beauty of the people and their land. The simplicity of rural Tanzania was deeply appealing, having spent all my life in the overly complicated Western world. I also discovered that despite the overwhelming odds the people had to struggle against, they maintained their dignity and self-worth. The hospitality of the poor was truly humbling. I promised myself I would return to Africa every year for the rest of my life. I had fallen in love.

On my return I was a mixture of raw emotion; outrage, compassion, anger, nihilism, and gratitude – all of which I carried into the schools programme. I channelled all these new experiences into the content of my material. But I was now questioning what I was doing and how I was doing it. More importantly, how did I really respond to the needs of the poor? I realized I needed to sharpen my focus, but how? I saw no value in starting another charity for the sake of it, as I was no longer sure the charity approach was the correct one. The non-profit money had created an artificial economy on the ground where I had been based in Tanzania that in turn had created a dependency culture. Where was the dignity in a begging bowl?

CHAPTER TWO

We met in November
And you kissed me so sweetly.
You cried as you told me
There was no bread to eat
So I brought you an ice cream
And watched your teeth scream

"Justice not Charity" became my slogan. Over the winter of 1993, I refocused the work under the name Christian Relief Education and Development, or CRED for short. My goal sharpened to engaging young people through both development education and campaigning, and also through holistic lifestyle changes. This seemed to me to be the only way I could move the work away from the delivery of intellectual knowledge, and root it in daily choices. For me, good campaigning meant three simple things: good education that leads to positive action, and then a change in lifestyle that cements campaigning into daily living.

This is where the fledgling Fairtrade movement proved so powerful; communicating fair trade principles to my audience became routine. All the young people I addressed were encouraged to lobby their schools to use Fairtrade products wherever possible. There is no doubt I upset a lot of dinner ladies and school accountants whose primary focus was cheap food, not Fairtrade.

The more I reflected on my trip to Tanzania, the more challenged I became about the structure one needed to deliver change. Our schools programme was legally defined under the charitable status of the local church. And its growing popularity meant we needed to expand it beyond our existing funding partner, Christian Aid. So I began to apply for financial support from Oxfam, Save the Children, and the European Union.

I found this often led to real challenges for some of the funding agencies, clearly confused by the idea of a local church delivering a socially empowering international justice message. They continually assumed we had an ulterior motive and really just wanted to convert people. The political correctness of some of the mainstream secular British development agencies at the time, I felt, was being used as a mask to avoid their own institutional discrimination. In most cases CRED would apply for a development education grant, could demonstrate a very high quality of delivery, yet fail to get funding on the grounds "We do not fund religious organizations". It was very frustrating.

My local church had been fantastic in getting me launched, and they had incubated the entire development education programme, but the new distinctive message of justice for the poor began to create a certain amount of tension in the Pioneer network of churches that my local church belonged to. For some of its leadership, achieving a national evangelical revival was the most important thing, and justice for the poor was a secondary outcome to a national spiritual revival. I did not agree.

This came to a head when I was asked to write an article in the network's magazine on "Where Justice Meets Revival".

In my article, I explained that the question was framed incorrectly. It was more about how a view of revival fitted in with God's commitment to the poor and the oppressed. I explained I was not an evangelical so a revival agenda was not my priority, and that the lifestyle of the church needed to reflect this commitment through campaigning, buying Fairtrade products, boycotting Nestlé, and giving away the church's wealth in service of the poor. The then leader of that network denounced my approach by writing a critical letter (under a pseudonym) expressing his concerns that I would slip off into heresy if I abandoned evangelicalism. Pursuing justice was viewed as a sexy message by sections of the broader church, but not a core activity. I felt like I was caught between a rock and a hard place. I was too Christian for the secular boys, and too secular for elements of the Christian fraternal.

In November 1994 I travelled to Ethiopia, as I had been asked by a leader of a church in Derby to contribute to a youth conference. He wanted me to talk about my work with CRED and our human rights education. It proved to be an important watershed for me, and also marked the beginnings of my relationship with the jewellery trade. The country had impacted me hugely during the mid 1980s, and the opportunity to visit was too good to turn down. Going to Ethiopia gave me the chance to make good on my promise to visit Africa every year, and also meant I would witness urban poverty in one of the poorest cities in the world, Addis Ababa.

Arriving in Addis was an explosion of emotion, an assault on the senses, and a harrowing of my consciousness. As we travelled around the city over the ten days of our trip, I struggled to take in the sheer complexity of life. Huge swathes of the city lived in abject destitution with little or no hope. I was numbed by the mass of human suffering on a scale I could not absorb. Every road junction we stopped at, we would be engulfed by a rugby scrum of children begging for food, three or four deep at our window. Women would offer us their children to take home, and the disabled pleaded for help with eyes full of sheer desperation. How could this be? In Tanzania the rural poverty had been acute and disturbing, yet here in Addis, the sheer number of people in the city meant the immediate impact of their poverty was magnified a hundredfold.

There simply was not enough emotional depth in my life to deal with this level of human suffering. I was reminded of Stalin's famous quote, "One death is a tragedy; one million is a statistic."

It is always easier to cope with the moral outrage and any sense of guilt if you can rationalize the enormity of the problem into a statistical set of numbers. I was well versed in the statistics via the United Nations Annual Development report, but numbers and statistics become irrelevant when faced with the spectre of death in the eyes of a malnourished child. Where was the hope? The Jesuit priest Jon Sobrino once said, "The highest authority on the planet is the authority of those who suffer, from which there is no appeal." I now understood what he was talking about.

Having been invited to contribute to a Christian youth conference on the Justice of God, I was struggling to deliver my material in the face of such daily suffering. I felt like a fraud. But my salvation came in the shape of Meron and Sarai, two street girls who were asking for me by name. "How can this be? I do not know any street girls," I wondered.

Naamen, our host and translator for the trip, knew both the girls and had told them that the team that I was a part of were in town. This at least explained how they were able to locate us, but I never did find out how they knew to ask for me by name. The girls began to tell me their story. Meron had been orphaned as a toddler. Both her parents had walked to Addis in 1985 during the famine and had died on the journey. Sarai's mother had abandoned her and her father was dead. Both the girls had been living on the streets behind the Ethiopia Hotel since they could remember, and were prostitutes. I made an educated guess that both girls were around eleven or twelve. Older boys regularly raped them. Their lives were violent, abusive, and loveless. Here were two little lives that had been tragically impacted by the famine of the mid eighties, the living legacy of a lost generation.

We took them for an ice cream, as they said they had never tasted one. The coldness of ice cream on their teeth was painful for them, and we all wept with laughter at the way they spooned it into their mouth, spat it out, and waited for it to melt so they could drink the slush from their bowls.

Having listened to them, I became very concerned for their welfare and wanted to take them to a doctor so they could get a health check and HIV test. Nick Pettingale, the leader of our team, told me to visit a woman called Sister Jember Teferra who ran a project in the four poorest slums in Addis called the Integrated Holistic Approach Urban Development Project (IHA-UDP). I would later discover why it was called this – "So the government or individuals cannot corrupt our approach to poverty alleviation," Jember informed me.

What she meant by this is that one of the biggest battles in any new organization is how to stop individuals – or in some cases, governments – from trying to take over a successful process and make it serve their own need for fame and fortune or a political agenda. Enshrining the approach to poverty alleviation in the name of the organization was one of Jember's ways of preserving the integrity of what they were doing on the ground with the poor.

Sister Jember's background explained even more. Everyone, including me, assumed she was a nun, because of her reputation as a campaigner and champion of the poor. In fact, her title of "Sister" referred to the nursing qualifications she had achieved on the wards of the National Health Service in the UK. Sister Jember was the niece of the emperor Haile Selassie, and had been educated in the UK in the 1950s and early sixties. After the military coup in 1974, the Dergue Regime had imprisoned her and her husband, and she had spent six years as a political prisoner. It was while in prison, as she tended to the needs of the dying and tortured prisoners, that she learned her approach to poverty alleviation.

I was profoundly moved by her story. Not only had she given up the privileges of her background, she had learned to forgive the regime that had imprisoned her and had emerged as a woman who would dedicate her life to the service of the needs of the poor. For her, poverty was not an abstract idea to be dealt with from the meeting rooms of development agencies and United Nations conferences hosted in five-star hotels. It was a daily reality to be engaged with, through compassion and social justice.

In its simplest terms, Jember's approach was a "felt needs" approach. Let the poor decide their own agenda; let them decide what needs to be done in their community, she thought. Don't assume you know better because you might have an education. The poor suffer poverty because authorities assume their political strategies are right for the country's economy, rather than for the people of the country. As an Orthodox Christian, Jember always saw the face of Jesus in the poor and suffering, and taught me to see the poor in the same way.

As I walked into her office with the two street girls in tow, I was greeted by a diminutive woman sitting at a desk, dwarfed by mountainous volumes of papers, reports, and books. I was invited to sit down and she looked at me quizzically with eyes of wisdom, forged in the heat of human suffering and undiminished compassion. We talked at length about her work and the empowerment approach she and her team took to poverty alleviation.

I explained I wanted her to arrange for health checks for Meron and Sarai. What she must have thought of this naive young man dumping two street kids on her, I have no idea, but I remember coming away from that encounter thinking how gracious she was in listening to my story. It would have been easy to turn them away on the grounds they did not live in the catchment area of the project, but she lavished time and attention on them both and promised to follow them up.

Jember then arranged for me to be driven to my guesthouse with one of the project drivers. On the way back, we dropped the two girls off behind the Ethiopia Hotel. They were by now in floods of tears. I told them that I would come back the following year and visit them.[1] As they walked back to their life on the streets, my body began to shake with raw emotion. I felt a surge of pain across my chest, as if my heart was being ripped from my body. The thought of those two girls returning to the daily horror of living and working on the streets was too much from me to imagine and I broke down in tears.

I now understood in a much more profound way what Jesus meant when he said the poor were members of his family.[2] I was having a visceral awakening to the presence of Christ in the poor, and it was very traumatic.

Ethiopia acted as a foundational training ground for me in understanding the needs of the poor and how to empower people. Jember was to become an excellent mentor over the next few years as she led by example, and to this day I see her as the Mother Teresa of Addis Ababa. "The day you no longer weep at the suffering of the poor is the day you need to stop," she once told me.

I began visiting Ethiopia every year and I would stay with Jember. I would also be adopted into her family as a result of a small dispute with the British Foreign Office.

On a scorching hot day in July 1994, Ruth and I had finally got married after a long engagement forced on us by her studies at Cambridge University. We had been seeing each other for over four years. The wedding was a low-key affair as neither of us had very much money. We decided to rent a school hall, gather family and friends around us for a huge buffet, and blow the main bit of the budget on a honeymoon in Malaysia. Both of us wanted to try to live as simply as possible as a way of outworking our commitment to justice and environmental issues.

Because I had been so moved by what I had seen on my first trip to Ethiopia, I was keen to have Ruth with me on my next trip in 1995. Toward the end of the trip, Ruth and I visited Lalibela, the town famous for its ancient rock-carved churches in the north of the country. Ruth unfortunately lost her passport, which meant a trip to the British Embassy to secure a travel document. The British Embassy complex is half a mountain equipped with all mod cons, and that included stables for the

Embassy official's wife's polo ponies. We were thrown out of the complex on her orders for "making the place look untidy".

On our return home to the UK, I wrote a facetious letter complaining about the exorbitant lifestyle of our embassy staff in the poorest country in the world, and demanded to know whether the playing of polo by British civil servants in Ethiopia was a good use of taxpayers' money. I asked the authorities to justify this behaviour and their lifestyles in the face of such abject poverty outside of the front door of our embassy, and suggested that perhaps we should sell off some of the land the embassy used and give the money to the poor.

Little did I know it would create such a storm. The Foreign Office called Addis Ababa immigration, who in turn called Jember's husband Haile-Giorgis, who used to be the mayor of Addis Ababa. He bounced it back to immigration saying it was an internal British matter. My Ethiopian friends found the whole incident very humorous and the idea of the British Embassy being used as a homeless shelter hysterical. I was duly labelled a troublemaker and welcomed into the fold.

During this 1995 visit I found Ethiopia enchanting: in a land of great beauty, awash with a rich culture, arts, crafts, and a unique jewellery tradition. The Coptic knotwork was very reminiscent of Celtic designs, with its own ethnic twist. Given that the Celtic motif was very in vogue at that time, I guessed it might sell when I got home. My aim was just to cover my flight costs. So I bought a few heavy white Ethiopian blanket-cum-shawls called Gabis, some Coptic jewellery, and a few pieces of pottery, and decided upon my return I would add them to the Tanzanian batiks I was now selling, to see if my commercial hunch was correct.

On the morning we were due to leave, a British expat called Yvonne knocked on Jember's door and asked to see me. She was a missionary working with a fledgling project called Women at Risk (WAR). WAR worked with prostitutes and their children, helping them, through counselling and vocational training, to get off the streets. She had heard I was buying jewellery and wanted to show me what the women she was working with had made.

Yvonne insisted I look at the product even though I tried to explain we were walking out of the door to go to the airport. "No" was not an answer she paid much attention to. She promptly produced a string of necklaces made from glass and copper beading threaded onto shoelaces. To be honest, they were a very poor quality stereotypical charity product. I knew they would never sell, but the story behind them moved me. I bought a few pieces, promised I would visit the WAR project properly when I returned next year, and flew home.

On the plane, I wondered, "Why did I buy that?" I concluded it was because the story moved me and my heart had won over my head. I began to understand that a powerful story was a really transformational element of a product. If you could couple a strong story with a quality product, you would have a winning combination.

The education work of CRED had been struggling for money for some time, so I took a gamble and hired Lucy Frazer, a young graduate dance teacher and artist, to develop the education programme with me. I needed help in delivering this as it was expanding and I was not a good organizer. If I did not get a better quality of person into the programme, I might blow it up through poor administration. Lucy was fantastic and took the programme on with the diligence and discipline of a dancing ninja. She introduced a justice and arts element that was brilliant and, between us, we added what would become CRED's flagship inter-school human rights conference. At its height under Lucy's leadership, the programme was reaching close to 50,000 young people across the south coast of England.

This released me to invest more into the international relationships that were beginning to develop. We wanted CRED to build directly with Jember and her project, and to link up some of the UK schools we worked with to one of the slum schools that

Jember was trying to reinvigorate. Alongside that, to generate a little income for the charity, I had put a stall out at church meetings of all the goods I had brought back from Ethiopia and the batiks that I was still importing ad hoc from Robert Mollel in Tanzania. We effectively sold out and made a tidy sum of cash, so I began to do this on a regular basis.

Here was an opportunity to experiment with an idea that had been teasing me for some time: could business be the solution we were looking for to alleviate poverty? I was struck by the consistency of the conversations I was having with slum dwellers in Addis. They all told me that they did not want charity handouts, they wanted a job so they could have the dignity of paying their own rent and feeding their own family. It was such a compelling request, rooted in the dignity of the individual and concern for their family's well-being. Perhaps we should start a company, buy goods from artisans and community-based groups, sell them for a profit, and reinvest this into the education work? We could create a virtuous economic circle of wealth creation and social transformation. This to my mind was the heart of the fair trade ethic: a business that had economic justice for the poor as one of its core activities. It was a great idea, but how should we do it?

In February 1996 a good friend of mine, Jon Pelley, and I launched Cred Trading Company. Jon was a relic of the 1970s punk generation made good. He was slightly anarchic and enjoyed thinking outside the box. I first met him when Ruth was at Cambridge; he was the leader of a student society that she attended. He moved to Chichester to be a part of the local church Ruth and I were part of, and proved very supportive of CRED's work. To earn a living, Jon had started a jewellery barrow in Portsmouth, and his knowledge of silver jewellery would prove invaluable as the company began to grow.

We started by capitalizing on increasing opportunities to speak and contribute in churches and conferences. Throughout the summer, most Christian denominations and Independent Church networks would hold annual festivals or events over a three- to four-day period. I had revamped the material we offered in schools to work with a more overtly Christian audience, and the groups seemed to like it. At the back of our presentations would be our CRED stall of arts, crafts, and jewellery that we were now buying from our partners. The jewellery proved to be the most popular and profitable product we sold.

Young people loved the message of social justice and campaigning on behalf the poor. We challenged them to seek out the poor in their own locations, raise money for overseas work, and write to the government on why the UK was not meeting the international target to give 0.7 per cent of its income to International Development. For a period of time we became the fashionable fringe in certain sections of the church.

I was stereotyped as an angry young man on a mission. I would often swear when getting my point across, and this got me into trouble with the more conservative elements of church leadership. I was more than happy to challenge the priorities of a church that put its own structure and institution before the needs of the poor and oppressed. This intentionally provocative approach confirmed I was an unpredictable maverick, and Jon or Lucy, on more than one occasion, had to write letters or cover for me, apologizing for my "unChristian" behaviour.

I found it strange that people would be more upset by swear words than by the unnecessary death of a child every six seconds and our numbness to our complicit participation in such an evil reality. Those of us working in CRED were moved by the truth of global injustice and how the voodoo economic structural adjustment policies of the IMF, World Bank, and our own international leaders were a part of creating such unjustifiable suffering around the world. Our heroes became those individuals that stood up against the prevailing winds of injustice; the South African anti-apartheid movement of Biko, Mandela, and Tutu, and the spiritual heavyweights such as Mother Teresa and the murdered Catholic bishop Oscar Romero.

It felt like the wind was in our sails and we were having an impact on the young groups of people with whom we were working. We were active participants of the early Fair Trade Movement, we promoted the Jubilee 2000 campaign to cancel Third World debt, we worked with Jubilee Action on child sex tourism issues, and we supported the World Development Movement. Alongside this we had forged a direct partnership in Addis Ababa with Jember Teferra's work. We had managed to find a way of delivering our message to a schools and student audience as well as a more Christian one. The challenge before us now was "How do we grow what we are doing?"

Over the next two to three years we worked very hard. Lucy continued to grow the education work and began to involve volunteers. Tracey Hutchings, our first volunteer, moved to Haringey in north London where she joined a local multicultural church called Rainbow that worked with refugees and the urban poor in London. She had been impacted by our message of justice for the poor and began a human rights group in a local pub near Wood Green. Eventually she would open a second CRED education office, come on-staff, and expand the programme. She also networked with UNICEF, who had some funding and education resources on the rights of the child. Although we never really fitted with UNICEF's institutional approach to the world, they were very happy to be able to access our growing network of schools across north London and the south coast, so the partnership worked well.

Lucy and Tracey between them became a dynamic duo of creative talent. The cross pollination of ideas and cultures enriched our education outreach and made us even more attractive to schools.

Meanwhile Jon and I focused on developing the business. I was now regularly travelling to Ethiopia and Tanzania, sourcing new products, and trying to build up a fair trade offering of goods that would be desirable, attractive, and good quality. The challenge we had was two-fold. We did not have any money to invest into the business and neither of us was very clear on how to develop a fair trade company. We were, however, convinced we had a good idea and we focused our energies on getting our business proposal in front of as many people as we could.

By the late 1990s, CRED had become an established part of the national festival circuit. Every summer we would travel around as many gigs as we could book, including Greenbelt, Soul Survivor, Stoke Newington Street Fair (where we had our entire takings for the day stolen), Strawberry Fair (before which the trailer-cum-stall we had hitched to Jon's car disintegrated at 60 mph on the M11), and the WOMAD world music festival.

Through doing these events, Jon and I worked out that the fair trade market was being flooded with handmade artisan crafts such as baskets, carvings, rugs, and batiks. The competition was becoming more intense, as every international development agency now had their own catalogue of ethnic arts and crafts and Fairtrade certified products, so why be just another retailer of what everyone else was doing? The wider consumer market was still quite suspicious of the idea of fair trade, as it had a popular image of being a movement of leftovers from the sixties who had cut their hair but still wore hemp underwear, were recalcitrant socialists, read the *The Morning Star*, and were waiting for the proletarian revolution.

As the most profitable side of the new business was jewellery, we decided to focus on developing a fair trade jewellery business. Jewellery was a lot easier to import from overseas, as I could put it in my suitcase. This worked well from Tanzania. Ethiopian customs, however, ran a scam at the airport. They would wait for you to board the plane and then, ten minutes before you were due to taxi down the runway, would call you off the plane, take you down to where the luggage was loaded, open your case, and inform you that the jewellery you had purchased did not have the right documents. They would then confiscate it if you did not bribe them. When you protested, they threatened to make you miss your plane while they redid the paperwork. I lost a lot of jewellery to this scam in the very early days of the business.

On one memorable occasion I had an irate Lufthansa pilot shouting out of the door of the plane for me to get back on board as we were late for take-off. I learned quickly that if you wore the jewellery no one would stop you, and if you wore a football shirt, you were more likely to end up in a discussion on the English Premiership than the contents of your bag. I also insisted that my travel companions wear the jewellery out of the country. We must have looked a very comical sight, walking through Addis Ababa airport with enough jewellery on our persons to make Mr T jealous.

As with most significant developments in my story, help found me rather than the other way around. Our little business was beginning to hit a natural ceiling, as there are only so many festivals you can do each summer, and the back of church meetings was not exactly the most dynamic retail environment in which to build a business. So when in 1998 the offer came in from David Murden to open an upstairs jewellery store in his Chichester shop, I jumped at the chance.

David Murden was a captivating individual who had started a small chain of high-street stores called And Albert World Crafts across the UK. He was soon to open his sixth store at 24 South Street, Chichester. David was umbilically linked to the idea of business as the means of delivering social transformation and justice for the poor. He travelled extensively in the Far East, including Cambodia, Vietnam, and Malaysia – as well as in West Africa – and had an exceptional eye for the essential beauty in a product.

His passion for local artisan craftsmanship and traditions taught me the true meaning of this word. He saw the artisan as the custodian of traditional cultures, and the artists as those who, through the craftsmanship of their hands, provided an authentic way for people around the world to enjoy the true genius of human creativity. David was clear that the race to make more profit, mechanize the means of production, reduce costs, and improve industrial efficiency was killing local indigenous cultures, and he was keen through And Albert to find a way of preserving this vast reservoir of cultural heritage and tradition.

His outlook was an eye-opener for me, and one I was very sympathetic toward. He was very encouraging of the idea of CRED outworking its desire to explore some of these fair trade principles in jewellery in his Chichester store.

Here was a man, eccentric and as obsessed with the same idea of regenerating the economies of poorer communities through trade as I was, who had been building his business for a lot longer than we had. He was never happier than when he was rooting around in some bazaar off the beaten track, sipping coffee, buying arts and crafts, filling containers, importing and distributing through the network of his shops, and selling a little bit of global genius to the British public. In David I saw a man I could learn from, and he became an early influence on what would become CRED Jewellery.

On the back of an envelope, I worked out that to take on the room above And Albert in Chichester, I would need £15,000. We had a small amount of cash that would cover the set-up costs, plus the stock we currently had, but needed to find at least another £8,000 to buy the silver jewellery required to fill out the new shop floor. I approached the Co-operative Bank, who CRED was banking with at the time, and presented my idea for an ethical fair trade jewellery company.

In the most uncooperative way, they dismissed the idea as ridiculous and not something they were interested in. Here I was, trying to develop an ethical business, and the bank that claimed to support ethical business was not interested. All I needed was a small loan of £6,000 as I had already negotiated credit terms with some jewellery suppliers.

So I walked into HSBC in Chichester, asked to see a business manager, presented the same idea, and after a very short discussion they offered me a new business account, credit card facility, and a £2,000 overdraft.

In the winter of 1999, armed with a paintbrush, some wholesale jewellery catalogues, my credit card, a new bank, and the measurements of our upper room, I started the process of transforming a bare space into a jewellery shop. By Christmas, we were open and I was entering another incarnation as the shopkeeper. CRED Jewellery was a pragmatic mixed bag of jewellery from Ethiopia and Tanzania that we had sourced ourselves, and contemporary modern designs from some of the more mainstream wholesale jewellery suppliers in the UK. I was acutely aware that we would not have been able to sustain a proper shop purely from our jewellery partners in Africa, so I took the decision to mix our jewellery products up.

We had a really encouraging start. Our range of ethnic mixed with contemporary modern jewellery meant we appealed to a wider range of customers, and being located inside the And Albert store meant we benefited from the overall feel-good factor that they generated through their ethical and fair trade approach to business. We also began to supply some of the other And Albert stores with a small concession range of jewellery. It all seemed too good to be true and our first year was a great success.

Standing at the top of the stairs, just outside the door to our little upstairs room, meant you could hear whoever was on the phone at the bottom of the short staircase. One morning, I overheard the And Albert shop manager discussing the financial situation And Albert were in. It was a tense, difficult conversation, fuelled with anxiety and defensiveness. It seemed that the chain had expanded too quickly and had a major cash flow crisis. They were "over-trading". I had no idea what that meant, so I found myself a business dictionary and read: "transacting more business than the firm's working capital can normally sustain, thus placing serious strain on cash flow and risking collapse or insolvency".

Did this mean that, after investing what little money we had as a very small business, we were about to lose our shop? To compound my anxiety, Lucy told me that she wanted to move on from running the education work: a double blow. How could I replace her? How would we meet the expectations of the schools that relied on our programme to meet their National Curriculum requirements? Also, Ruth announced that she was pregnant with our first child.

I was now excited as well as anxious about the future. It made me realize that despite all the work done in setting up the charity and company, we were still a very small and vulnerable outfit.

CHAPTER THREE

The jewellery industry has got its head so far up its own arse on ethical issues it's swinging on its own tonsils.

The turn of the millennium would prove significant, not just for CRED and me but for the jewellery industry as whole. The scandals surrounding the funding of civil wars and rebel army groups through the illicit trade in diamonds was a breaking story. The African nations of Sierra Leone, Angola, and the Democratic Republic of the Congo were all suffering from wars and rebel insurgencies that were being funded in no small way by the mining, smuggling, and selling of rough diamonds to the international market. These diamonds became known as blood diamonds, and the big diamond companies and the international bourses who trade in rough diamonds were caught with their trousers down, profiting from the proceeds. The response to this conflict problem would be the introduction of the Kimberley Process, a set of international customs procedures that could ban the movement of rough diamonds from certain countries that were suffering from wars and conflicts.

But I was more preoccupied with saving the fledgling little silver jewellery company that we had started. With And Albert in the grip of impending bankruptcy and a new Creditors Voluntary Agreement being implemented, I could sense the writing was on the wall. Walking home one late afternoon from another day in the upper room, I noticed a new "for lease" sign up over the Hoover shop at 41 South Street. I made the call, got the details, offered £500 more than the annual rent, talked to the bank, extended the overdraft, and put in an offer. Within a matter of days the landlord came back with a yes. We were moving again.

I called Jon to let him know. He was now in the grip of training to become a teacher, but he still did the odd day in the shop for me, along with our newest part-time staff member, Reuben Pope. We handed in our notice and, after a month of painting in the evenings and our spare time, we closed on a Saturday evening, walked the cabinets the 500 yards down the road, and opened for business on the Monday morning.

The transition to a bigger high-street shop was a big step for me. It was very exciting and daunting at the same time. I was acutely aware that I had no formal business background and suffered from a lack of experience in the general process and administration required to keep a company moving forward. I get bored very easily, and concentrating on the detail required to run a business was not a strong point for me at the time. Also, all the demands that this brought meant I could no longer invest myself into the education side of the work.

So we reconstituted the education work of CRED into its own charitable foundation and I became a trustee. This removed me from being operationally involved, much to the relief of the staff – and myself. I was now free to focus exclusively on building up the business. Lucy had arranged to replace herself with another graduate teacher, another Lucy, Lucy Pendlebury, who would work alongside Tracey and Reg Hawkes, the office manager. Coupled with the continual stream of volunteers, the programme continued to grow and flourish. One of these volunteers was Christian Cheesman, a design graduate from Portsmouth University, who would become a real help as the company grew.

At the end of May 2000, Mali-Grace was born. I was now a father. I was delighted. Having a newborn baby was wonderful even if, like most new parents, I was unsure of what to do. Ruth settled into being a fantastic mum and, despite the sleepless nights and pervasive smell of dirty nappies throughout the house, the summer evenings holding Mali in the garden with the scent of jasmine hanging in the air became moments of serenity and reflection in what remained an intensely challenging growth time for us. The small child in my arms constantly reminded me of two of the most important things in life – purity and innocence.

The most significant development for the business's mission resulted from a trip that Christian and I took to Jaipur, India in early 2001. Having already begun travelling in India the previous year, I had established a relationship with a few Delhi-based jewellers who supplied us with Indian rope chains, necklaces, and bracelets. But in all my discussions with these suppliers they had all talked about Jaipur as being the centre of the Indian jewellery industry. I decided that we should explore Jaipur as, through my research, I had learned that it touches almost all the coloured gemstone jewellery manufacturing in India. I was keen to explore the prospects of setting up our own special supplier relationship. So, armed with the address of the Evergreen Guesthouse in Jaipur, Christian and I set off to find our first fair trade supplier.

At that time, the idea of fair trade in jewellery was not on the customers' radar. Apart from the ethnic craft jewellery, which is where I had started with pieces from Ethiopia and Tanzania, no one had tried to put the words "fair trade jewellery" together, or asked what this would look like. My journey thus far had taught me that ethnic jewellery was a limited low value niche market, and that mainstream customers didn't buy poor quality, unfashionable jewellery. What they wanted was contemporary modern designs, well-crafted and affordable. The level of consumer awareness around ethical issues in jewellery was almost zero at the time, and consumers simply did not ask questions about the source of their jewellery.

Another issue was that the UK had strict laws in place regarding the quality and purity of the jewellery that could be bought and sold. Silver jewellery had to be a minimum of 92.5 per cent pure silver to qualify for the silver hallmark. I had discovered that many of the fair trade craft companies, selling what they called fair trade jewellery, were in fact selling illegally. What they called silver was in fact an alloy metal that looked like silver. Fair trade in the jewellery sector at the turn of the millennium meant that the piece had been made by a small cooperative somewhere, supporting women's groups or an orphanage. In short, it was a charity purchase and however important that charitable work was, it was never going to be taken seriously in a jewellery industry dominated by luxury brands and transnational mining companies.

Jaipur is known as the Pink City, because most of its buildings are painted that colour. It is intensely beautiful and, at sundown, as the sun kisses the edge of the Rajasthan desert, the canvas of reds and oranges reflects off the pink of the buildings, and the transcendent mystery that is India washes you with glory. I was immediately taken in by the romance of the place.

Arriving in Jaipur bus station after an overnight journey from Delhi's totally mad bus terminal was a relief. We climbed down onto the concrete floor and breathed in the noise, the heat, the dust, the colour, the mayhem, the smells, and the electric atmosphere that is urban India. We were instantly surrounded by the usual hustlers, trying to take us to guesthouses. We choose one guy who spoke relatively good English and headed off to the Evergreen.

As we dodged and weaved our way across town by tuk-tuk, the motorized three-wheeled taxi used across Asia, we explained why we were in Jaipur, what our business was, and our driver offered to help. We learned that all the tuk-tuk drivers are linked to the labyrinthine commercial networks that spread across the city. They know everyone and everything that is going on, and we were fortunate our new-found friend was willing to help our search for a good jewellery manufacturer. As he dropped us at the Evergreen, we arranged to meet him again the next day. The following morning, our new friend boldly told us that he wanted to take us to a place on the edge of town near the Jai Mahal (Lake Palace), where a man had a jewellery emporium.

Mansoor Khan ran the Jewels Lake Palace Emporium and was also an established dealer in gemstones. Outside his shop sat a number of older men, using a grinding wheel to cut and polish small stones. Khan's store was a treasure trove of gorgeous Indian-style jewellery, set with every coloured gemstone you could imagine. I felt like a pirate who had discovered a hidden treasure chest. But if Mansoor was to become one of our ongoing suppliers, I wanted to know about labour conditions during manufacturing and in the mines that the stones came from. Clearly these discussions were sensitive.

I was satisfied through conversation and observation that he did not employ children and the conditions for his workers were good. But what about the stones themselves? Where did they come from? I pressed him on this issue and hit a wall. He was not talking; evidently this was a question that he had never been asked before.

That night, Christian and I decided that we needed a different approach to getting the information. We would lay out on the table all the jewellery that we were going to buy from him, and then explain that unless he arranged for us to visit the local gemstone mine, we would not make the purchase. Mansoor was clearly uncomfortable with being pressured, but the lure of a big sale was a strong motivator. He asked for some time to arrange it and promised he would get back in touch soon.

This gave us the time to explore the underbelly of the Jaipur jewellery industry. Jaipur is the centre of a coloured gemstone web fed by many countries – rubies from Burma, sapphires from Sri Lanka, stones from Madagascar, lapis lazuli from Afghanistan, amber from Africa, and much more. It is estimated that Jaipur has in excess of 60,000 workers in the gemstone industry, of which over 10,000 are children.[1] Given that we were European buyers who looked unofficial (or scruffy), and that Christian had a wonderfully disarming approach to small talk (something I have never mastered), we were able to access the rooms above shops, stores, and at the back of houses that represented the alter ego of the Jaipur's jewellery world.

We discovered the home-based workers who, for a few rupees, threaded beads, faceted stones, and hand-polished silver. Most of our hosts were not stupid: they knew that child labour was illegal and deeply unpopular with Westerners, so, often as we were shown around small factories, there would be certain rooms with closed doors. When we asked what happened behind them, we would be told the rooms were private. Eventually we worked out that if Christian went ahead and talked to our hosts, I could hang back and, without permission, open side doors and look inside. On more than one occasion I would see children's tiny hands cutting and polishing tiny stones in darkened rooms. It was more than Dickensian in look and feel. I felt as though we were walking through a surreal movie set, except this was no stage production; this was life in the raw. Jaipur was beginning to show us its more unpleasant side.

After three days of constant negotiation with Mansoor, a car turned up in the morning to pick us up. We were off to visit a mine south of Jaipur on the Mumbai road. The car was uncomfortably small, and travelling into the desert felt more like the Dakar Rally than a business trip. After about two hours, we suddenly veered off the road and drove two miles to what looked like a deserted village, with broken-down slum dwellings. As we opened the doors, the suffocating heat of Rajasthan's desert hit us full in the face.

It was unbearable; we were in 100°F of heat. Our guide beckoned to us to follow him up a hill and, as we walked, he introduced us to the mine owner, a small man who shook our hands and said very little throughout the rest of the trip. As we walked, I got talking to one of Mansoor's staff. He explained that this site was a garnet mine from which they bought rough stone to be polished and used in their jewellery. It used to be owned by a bigger mining operation that had recently sold it to the new owner. He also explained that there used to be a pipeline that supplied water to the makeshift dwellings that acted as the mineworkers' homes. When the old owner left, he dismantled the water pipe, leaving the little village and its workers with no clean water, and reliant on being supplied with bottled water by the new owner at great expense to the miners as it was deducted from their wages.

As we reached the brow of the not inconsiderably sized hill, it abruptly stopped. It was in fact only half a hill. Below me was a vertical drop of some twenty to thirty metres straight down. At its base was a huge pit where the miners worked with simple tools, clawing at the face of the hill to extract the rough garnets. We walked down to the pit and saw the extremities that these miners were subjected to every day: the heat, rock, thirst, and the Neolithic working conditions. It was horrific. I felt like I was looking at the gateway to hell, and like Dante, whom I was reading at the time, I was overcome with the desolation of the moment.

> *Through me the road to the city of desolation,*
> *Through me the road to sorrows diuturnal,*
> *Through me the road among the lost creation.*[2]

The heat was unbearable. We turned back to the small village, seeking shelter from the unremitting penetration of the sun. As we sat down to take a drink, an old lady came over to me and indicated she wanted to talk. Through our guide, she explained that she and her children were miners who worked on this site. They were very poor. In fact, they owed the landowner money, an inherited debt from the previous owner, and most of the little they earned went back to paying off this debt. The pittance that was left was spent on rice and water. For this family and the dozens that worked this site, the gates of hell had closed behind them and they had become another statistic.

That night all I could do was weep at this unknown injustice. How had I missed this issue in all my work on human rights? My sorrow turned to blinding anger as I realized the acute dishonesty of the jewellery profession. The marketing story, created through advertising and publicity, was one of luxury and beauty; yet where was the beauty in such extreme forms of slavery, exploitation, and cruelty, and its direct association to my industry? This moment of lucid clarity was an epiphany for me. I suddenly saw the fullest extent of the challenge before us if we were to fulfil the goal the company had set in becoming a fair trade jeweller.

My total ignorance of small-scale mining was a deep embarrassment to me. Equally disturbing was the fact that no one in the jeweller sector had, to my knowledge, bothered to address its scandalous abuses. Clearly the barren soullessness I had witnessed in the desert was also true of the child labour conditions I had seen in the back rooms of Jaipur's cutting and polishing sector. The walk up that hill of desolation became a symbol to me of the extent of the mountain we needed to climb to demonstrate justice in the jewellery sector.

So began a frenetic attempt to understand what was going on in the jewellery supply chain. I was confused over what to do about the issues I had seen India. I knew that despite my moral outrage and the veracity of the eyewitness account that I had, these would not be enough to convince an industry there was a problem. In the few conversations I had had with industry bodies at the time, all my ethical aspirations had been batted back, with the general consensus being that I was mad trying to get an ethical product to market. "Impossible" was the standard reply. Nor was I 100 per cent clear on what ethical jewellery should look like.

I knew I needed an empirical academic research document to back up what I had witnessed. I needed to understand the full extent of the problem. Now I had looked into the ethical hole in the industry, how far down did it go? The challenge was where to go to get this work done, and exactly what did I want researching?

I had been hanging around the Body Shop HQ in Littlehampton. My search for relevant business models to copy had taken me to their doors as they were the country's leading campaigning commercial company at the time. They had set up their community trade department in the late nineties and had employed a Canadian, Jacqui MacDonald, to shape, systematize, and implement their work with their international suppliers. She proved to be a huge source of help and wisdom to me during those formative years, sharing key material on how the Body Shop did their community trading, and how they integrated their ethical position into a commercial company without compromising the needs of the business.

I was deeply impressed by their policy of never paying for advertising and the way they invested the equivalent amounts of money into their community trade partners, and used their campaigning as their key voice to market.

The CRED education work had often backed the Body Shop's human rights campaigns, such as the unsuccessful protests against the 1995 state execution by hanging of Nigerian Ken Saro-Wiwa over his defence of the Ogoni people against the corporate violence and environmental destruction meted out by the Shell Corporation. I explained to Jacqui what I had seen in India and what I needed to have researched. She recommended speaking to the Natural Resources Institute (NRI), which was linked to the University of Greenwich in London.

The NRI was very positive about the idea and, after I had briefed them on the scope of the research I wanted, they put a clear proposal together and gave me the price tag of £10,000. I wanted the NRI to research the silver supply chain, as at the time CRED was primarily a silver and coloured gemstone jewellery company. We wanted to know what the supply chains looked like for this aspect of the industry. What were the main countries feeding the international silver supply chain? What were the percentage of small-scale miners to large-scale miners in the industry, and the environmental impacts of this process? How did the material travel around the world, who processed it, how was it processed, and what was the legacy that the process had on the lives of the poor?

I recognized that we needed to move CRED from being an aspirational ethical jewellery business, based on first-hand assurances, to delivering an ethical jewellery product in quantifiable ways. So we asked for recommendations on what a small ethical jewellery company could look like and what kind of proofs we would need to back up any claims. Ann Tallontire, one of the NRI researchers, recommended I go to the UK government's Department for International Development and talk to the extraction industries desk, to see if they would back the research project. Amazingly, they stumped up half the cash and, with the CRED Foundation putting in the other half, we secured the budget. So began the UK's first comprehensive analysis of the supply side of the jewellery trade. All we could do now was wait the twelve months for the report to be delivered in early 2003.

Upon my return from the India trip, I received a call from Jember in Ethiopia saying that the government was going to forcibly evict 135,000 people from their homes, so a Malaysian company, Adorna Alfa, could build a retail park and luxury homes. She wanted me to coordinate the UK campaign to respond to this outrage. If it went ahead, hundreds of thousands of pounds of British money from groups such as Comic Relief, Band Aid, and other national and international agencies would be bulldozed away, creating untold misery for the tens of thousands of the poorest of the poor.

I am a biker at heart, and returning home on my Triumph Bonneville from a speaking engagement in Herne Hill, I was hit by a car. I remember saying to myself, as I ploughed into the driver-side door of the car that pulled out in front of me, "When you hit the road, roll." For the few seconds as I cartwheeled through the air over the top of the offending car, my mortality became the biggest presenting issue in my life.

Fortunately the car behind me was being driven by an off-duty nurse, and within minutes an off-duty ambulance arrived on the scene. They dosed me up with gas and air and transported me, as high as a kite, to hospital. There, after X-rays, I was informed I had a seriously shattered wrist and would have to be in the hospital for forty-eight hours. Surgery would be the following day, with a further day of observation required.

Disaster! I was due to meet with singer-songwriter and activist Bob Geldof in two days' time to talk about the Adorna Alfa situation in Ethiopia. It had taken weeks to set this meeting up. There was no way I could miss it. Not only did I care passionately about the pioneering work of Jember and her team, some of the poor artisan jewellers we still bought from lived in this part of Addis Ababa. The doctors just did not see it my way, saying they had a strict policy that after a general anaesthetic I needed a 24-hour observation period. I asked if they could do the surgery with a local anaesthetic and, if so, could I check out the following day? Yes, they could, but it was not normal practice for a break this severe.

I insisted on a local anaesthetic, so in the morning they wheeled me into surgery. After an hour of grinding, yanking, twisting, drilling, and further brutalizing of my arm, the surgeon announced that everything was back in its correct alignment, pinned, set, and plastered. All that remained for me to do was come back in eight weeks to have the cast removed, and to talk to the anaesthetist about immediate pain relief.

The very camp anaesthetist explained it was far better for me to have an anal suppository, as once my arm woke back up, it would be very painful. I took the good medical advice and the gentleman in question slapped on a pair of rubber gloves, shoved his finger where the sun never shines, announced the successful launch of my next twelve hours of pain relief, and minced off out of the surgery.

The next day I met Geldof on the King's Road, where he laughed that "wanking is off the menu for the next few months". We duly got down to talking about how we could stop this ridiculous bulldozing of the slums by the Malaysians.

Given what we had witnessed in Rajasthan, we decided to stop buying from Jaipur. This was not an easy decision to take, as I wanted to stay in there and work with the industry to reform the process, but practically, CRED was not big enough, either personnel-wise or financially, to take on such a huge project.

The company was doing OK; Chichester was performing well, but our second shop in Wood Green Shopping Centre, opened six months previously, was proving problematic. The demographic of the area meant that the "spend per head" on jewellery was lower than Chichester. Also, continual issues around staffing meant we were constantly fighting fires with non-attendance and unprofessionalism. It was a constant drag on our ability to make profit.

Now that Jaipur had proved unworkable for us, we still had an ambition to find a silver jewellery cooperative that could produce good quality contemporary designs that also fulfilled our desire to create a more fair trade offering in jewellery.

After a morning of searching on the Internet and talking to the trade attaché from the Nepalese embassy, I managed to get a list of about a dozen artisan businesses in Kathmandu that had email addresses. I sent them all an outline of what CRED Jewellery was looking for in a jewellery trade partner, and waited for a reply. Hari Thapa of New Nepalese Global Industries was the only person to return my email. Although his English was not great (and why should it be?), there was enough of a description about his company to give me hope that this might be an opportunity worth exploring.

One of the greatest delights and privileges afforded me with jewellery was the travel. It became a glorious distraction from the more mundane side of running the business. It also became a rich source of story through which I could help our customers to see what the challenges were in securing ethical jewellery for them.

The flight to Nepal was uneventful, but my first view of the Himalayas was humbling and I began to cry. The vista was immense and the grandeur deeply moving. As we swept down the Kathmandu Valley toward the airport, the excitement in me grew at the chance of using jewellery to see a modicum of justice established through an ethical trading partnership.

I had arranged to meet with Hari Thapa at the airport entrance. As I walked down the airport road, past soldiers, tanks, and machine-gun positions, I guessed all was not well with the politics of the country. I would later learn that the Maoist insurgency against the divine authority of the king of Nepal was in full swing.

Hari and his family greeted me by draping a garland of orange flowers around my neck. It was a beautiful greeting, full of honest pleasure, sincerity and joy. I liked him instantly. He drove us back to his house, where we had lunch, and then on to the hotel where I would be staying.

Hari Thapa was the founder and manager of the small silver cottage industry. He had married Yamuna Bajracharya twenty years earlier. She belonged to the Newar Community, a very old ethnic clan in the Kathmandu Valley. The Bajracharya are well known in Nepal for their traditional occupation of making ornaments and jewellery. Yamuna had been making silver jewellery from a young age, so she had a special relationship with it, and her filigree work was exceptional.

The following day we talked about our respective businesses and Hari showed me around his small operation. His workshop had been established by his father and now employed over fifteen silversmiths from across the city and outlying villages. He paid them a living wage, and provided schooling for some of their kids. The working conditions were very good, well ventilated, and each jeweller had his own bench to work from. The designs I showed him were well within the capability of his artisan smiths to make. I saw in Hari Thapa a partner CRED could work with for the foreseeable future, and we worked on putting some bangle designs into production.

I also visited a box manufacturer, one of the Body Shop's oldest community trade partners. As they showed me the before and after effect of working with the Body Shop, I got a glimpse of what we might be able to achieve through developing long-term relationships with guys such as Hari. They had established a community school, a reforestation programme, an agricultural project that fed the families associated with the business, and also provided employment for well over a hundred workers.

This trip was turning out to be a breakthrough for us. Not only had we taken a step forward in our desire to be more involved with the manufacturing of our jewellery, we had also found a sustainable and green source of packaging. For me the story was developing, but there was still the one outstanding question I could not get an answer to. Where did the silver come from? When I quizzed Hari on this point, he was very honest. He bought it from Standard Charter Bank in 1 kilo bars. He had no idea where the bank got it from and, when I encouraged him to ask the question, he was reluctant to create waves. He could not afford to lose his bullion account with them and it would have been churlish to insist.

CRED was making huge strides as a small jeweller; we now had good experience of sourcing from different African suppliers, we had explored the underbelly of the Indian jewellery trade in Jaipur and witnessed the exploitation there was in manufacturing and gemstone mining, and we had worked out how to develop ethical trading relationships with artisan manufacturers. We were beginning to understand the human rights and environmental issues in the jewellery supply chain, but I was also acutely aware and frustrated at our inability to get more transparency and traceability in the precious metal supply chain. We still could not break the wall of silence regarding the source of the metals. The banks would not return phone calls, the bullion houses would not answer questions, and all our suppliers gave us the same response that Hari did: "It all comes from the banks." I felt like we had hit a ceiling on how far we could go, and my frustration was beginning to boil over.

Coupled to my frustrations around understanding the complexities of the ethical challenges in jewellery, Wood Green was still not performing and we had to accept that if we did not resolve this issue soon, it might very well put us out of business.

I had taken the step a year earlier of hiring a recommended business consultant to help in restructuring the business for growth. It proved to be a big mistake. Rather than helping us through a growth opportunity, this man became the straw that nearly broke the camel's back. He simply did not understand what we were trying to create as an ethical jewellery company. All he understood was a narrow philosophy of reducing costs, squeezing suppliers, extracting more work from employees, and making sure his expenses were paid on time.

As a team, we knew what we had to do to save the company from collapse. Close Wood Green, make the staff redundant, and sack the consultant. I also took the unprecedented step of coming off the payroll. I wanted everyone to see I was going to lead from the front. CRED by now had become more than a business: it had become a mission that we all believed in, but the reality was if the landlord in Wood Green would not release us from our lease, we would have to go into administration. I genuinely thought we would lose the business and told Ruth to prepare for a torrid time while the whole thing unravelled.

CHAPTER FOUR

Jewellery is worn to beautify; there is no beauty in exploitation.

The year 2003 started under a cloud. Unsure if the company would make it through the upheavals of a severe restructure, I was now looking for a job to supplement the household income. We also had a second child on the way, the prospect of which added to the financial pressure for both of us. I was at one of my lowest moments to date. How would we survive?

It was very humbling for me. I had made some strategic mistakes based upon my own hubris, and Wood Green was the slap in the face I needed. I had taken my eye off the ball and I had only myself to blame.

Added to this, no one in the industry took us seriously and I found this really demoralizing. I felt like I was banging my head on a brick wall. Our wholesale suppliers liked us as a customer but did not really care about our ethical position. The most distressing aspect of my conversations with them was their patronizing attitude: "That's a real shame. We really admire what you are trying to do, but there is nothing we can do about it." I would stand at the bottom of my garden, stare up at the stars and shout, "Is this all there is?" Maybe the detractors were right. Perhaps what we wanted to achieve was very noble but genuinely impossible, and I needed to admit defeat.

A small ray of light emerged when our landlord in Wood Green said he would release us from our lease and gave us three months' notice to quit. Also, to pay the household bills, I took a part-time job with the Christian Socialist Movement as a membership officer.

By Easter, we had closed down Wood Green, and gone through the very unpleasant job of making the staff redundant. Christian, who had been on the payroll, had gone back to being self-employed and doing odd jobs for us. We were back to where we had started with one shop, a manager in Reuben Pope, a part-time shop assistant, and an increased overdraft that had paid for the costs of the closure of Wood Green. We did not have much to show for all our efforts to become an ethical jeweller.

It was during these dark months that I first met Anita Roddick. She was one of my heroes, along with Bob Geldof of Live Aid, and Katharine Hamnett, the award-winning campaigning fashionista. Anita had achieved all that I aspired to. I saw CRED Jewellery as the Body Shop of the jewellery world. She had heard about what we were trying to do through a mutual friend, Rachael Bentley, who was now running a Body Shop Foundation project called Children on the Edge.

I met Anita in a coffee shop over the road from the South Street shop, and she listened intently to my story. She asked lots of questions about me, my faith, my motivation, and what I hoped to achieve. I felt a total failure talking with her, given what had just happened with Wood Green. Here was the country's most successful social entrepreneur, with hundreds of shops around the world, a successful foundation funding cutting-edge projects, and I had one small silver jewellery shop with ethical suppliers in Nepal and a handful of ethnic jewellery suppliers from Ethiopia. But Anita was a very intuitive and empathetic person, and her maternal instinct obviously picked up on my dejected state. She was very encouraging, and talked about the early challenges of the Body Shop and how she had only set it up as a way of campaigning on issues she was passionate about.

"Greg, just tell the story," she said to me, as we parted company.

She gave me hope and the courage to keep going, and we would meet as regularly as possible over the coming years.

Published in July 2003, the NRI report entitled "Towards an Ethical Jewellery Business" was dynamite. I felt this report could inject the entire jewellery industry with the adrenaline shot it needed to wake up to the fact that it was standing on the backs of the poor and enriching itself from their misery. The report characterized the mining industry as broadly negative and challenged the well-crafted myth that large-scale mining had any positive social or environmental impact on poorer countries. It revealed the extent of child labour and social exploitation, and said that working conditions were bad within the diamond and gemstone industry.

The report also highlighted the big unknowns: the lack of transparency and accountability with traders, banks, and in the manufacturing of jewellery. Silver took a big hit because over 60 per cent of new silver coming to market was a by-product of other large-scale mined products such as zinc, lead, copper, and gold. These heavy industries were often (if not always) associated with poor waste management, groundwater contamination, acid rock drainage, and high levels of pollution from accessory metals, as well as forced relocations without free and informed prior consent of local or indigenous people.

The report demonstrated what a toxic foundation the jewellery world was built on. Admittedly there were a couple of international initiatives run by the International Labour Organization and World Bank that were seeking to address some of the extremes, but anyone like me who had a modicum of a community-based development background knew these processes were often top level, politically driven, and consultant-orientated, and often ended up serving the corporate institutions rather than the "felt needs" of the grass roots communities affected by mining. They would certainly not help small jewellers improve the ethical quality and transparency of the jewellery the customer was buying.

I phoned Michael Hoare, the Chief Executive of the National Association of Goldsmiths (NAG), and arranged a meeting to go through the report's findings and to see if NAG wanted to respond to the issues it contained. CRED had joined NAG because membership offered a preferential rate on our credit card fees. At the time it was the only benefit I could see of being a member.

Michael was very open at our meeting, but also realistic. He explained that NAG members (who numbered in excess of 900 jewellers) were, by and large, small independent family jewellers, whose knowledge of ethical issues was limited or non-existent. Customers at this time were simply not asking ethical questions about jewellery and, as a result, he would be surprised if many jewellers would be interested in what the report contained. However, there was a NAG council meeting that September, so would I be able to address the great and the good of the jewellery world in the UK? He offered me a twenty-minute slot and I agreed to do it, in the vain hope that the tide might start turning.

At home we were getting ready for the birth of our second child, due in early August. It was a hot summer and, with a stabilized business, Ruth and I were starting to think that perhaps we were through the difficult squeeze of the first half of the year. One morning Ruth got a phone call from a friend of hers who worked for Tearfund, one of the big three Christian development agencies in the UK. Apparently she had heard that I was trying to produce ethical jewellery. She knew of a woman, Catalina Cock Duque, who was in the UK trying to find support for a green gold programme in Colombia. My reaction was not hugely positive. Gold was not a product we touched: we simply could not afford to live in the luxury end of the jewellery world. This required lots of money – a commodity CRED was seriously short of.

The summer continued to be hot, and London was in full swing as I stood outside the Odeon cinema in Leicester Square.

I realized I had no idea what Catalina would look like, so when a young confident-looking woman came up and asked if I was Greg Valerio, whatever stereotype I had of a frumpy old hippy campaigner was instantly dispelled.

Catalina spoke extensively about her background as a young student, getting involved with advocating against the Pan American highway being built through the Chocó Pacific region of Colombia. The Chocó is one of South America's biodiversity hotspots, and the idea of putting a multi-lane concrete boulevard right through the middle of pristine rainforest was outrageous. Catalina had studied political science and sociology at the London School of Economics and became an anti-poverty campaigner after her first visit to the Chocó, where she witnessed the dreadful poverty and social and cultural marginalization of the Afro-Colombian people.

Significantly, on that first trip to Chocó, the light aircraft that she and her father were travelling in crashed. They both survived, but it forced her, as a young woman, to confront her own mortality and assess what she wanted to invest her life in. She was passionate in her plea on behalf of the Chocó miners.

"It's no use doing all the work on empowering local communities and preserving the environment if we cannot develop a market for the gold that our friends are mining," she told me. "If they do not make a living out of the process, the illegal miners will offer cash incentives to the communities for permission to destroy their environment by mining their gold."

I had a strong empathy for her and the work of Oro Verdé (Green Gold). Like us, they were battling against the odds; like us, no one really took them seriously; like us, everyone told them what they were doing was impossible. Like us, they had a dream of social, economic, and environmental justice for the communities, yet were struggling to get their idea launched. But I was also brutally honest with her, even though I was sympathetic and totally supported their idea. In fact, I was amazed at how they had managed to achieve anything at all. CRED Jewellery was a small business that focused on silver and coloured gemstones: we were not a big gold and diamond brand. We simply did not have the money to invest into gold. I did agree to an early visit to the Chocó in the next year. I was intrigued by the picture of a rich culture and ecosystem under threat by corporate and illegal interests.

September saw me attending my first NAG council meeting. I was nervous. I have never been comfortable at official functions. White wine, canapés, and meaningless small talk all add up to a boring experience for me. I was aware that the NRI report was potentially very damaging to the jewellery industry and its reputation.

At the reception preceding the meeting I was introduced to numerous individuals who eyed me up and down with a not too well-hidden air of suspicion. My deep-seated frustration at the industry's seemingly wilful ignorance of the big issues associated with our products had made me resolve to tell the truth and see what happened. I took Mike Morris with me for moral support. I felt a little like a Christian about to be thrown to the black-suited lions. If I was going to get eaten alive, it would be nicer to have a friend alongside me to witness the carnage.

Michael Hoare introduced me to a room full of middle-aged white men and left me to it. So I began.

I address you this morning as an activist and small businessman. As a result of this I often tread on the toes of individuals who are more specific in certain fields than I am. However, I came to be in the jewellery business because of my conscience, my commitment to fighting injustice and alleviating human suffering. Our industry is responsible for creating objects of intense beauty, but we also create intense suffering. This is not a moral position for us to hold.

I want to quote Geoff Field of the British Jewellery Association. "It is imperative that the integrity, not simply of our members, but of the entire jewellery supply chain is preserved."

When I started CRED Jewellery, I did so with one overarching ambition: to develop an ethical jewellery business that could supply customer demand for high quality, affordable, design-led jewellery that also addressed the social, environmental, and human rights issues that are present in our supply chain. For me it is not enough to give quality customer satisfaction when I know that the customer demand for a product may lead to the exploitation of another human being.

I talked at length about my experiences in India and Nepal, what I had witnessed in the manufacturing sector, and the plight of small-scale miners, and then continued:

The inherent value of our industry must be judged by the impact it has on the whole supply chain, from miners to customers. All share in the genius of our business. Jewellery is worn to beautify; there is no beauty in exploitation.

In recognizing that there are issues we face as an industry we must however be grounded in the veracity of the situation. I no more subscribe to the "shouting from the touchline about all things bad and business bashing" that some NGOs engage with than the "head in the sand – we actively discourage our members from talking about these issues as they will put us all out of business", which is a quote from one of the leading trade magazines in our industry.

Customers are increasingly more educated about their spending habits. Indeed the mantra "Vote with your wallet" has increasingly becoming the new democratic medium through which citizens express their personal choices and preferences. Customers are no longer just asking the question "What do you make or sell?" They are increasingly asking the question "How was it made? Who made it? How was it produced?" Examples are coffee (Café Direct), chocolate (Green & Blacks), cosmetics (Body Shop), cotton (Katharine Hamnett), diamonds

*(Kimberley Process) to name a few. It is only a matter of time
before consumer attention is turned on the jewellery industry.
I know that the Ethical Trading Initiative (ETI) were looking at
the jewellery [industry] but decided to focus their attentions on
the supply chain issues within the electronics [industry] instead.
I summarize some of the findings emanating from our research
programme with the NRI.*

I went on to give an exhaustive list of the findings and the direct
impact jewellery was having on the environment, human rights,
and labour standards: its complicity with bonded slave labour,
and political and financial corruption from the mine site upward.
I made the point that

*a more comprehensive read of the report will add fuel to the fire
that jewellery as a whole has some seismic social, environmental,
human rights, and livelihoods issues it needs to face up to.*

The atmosphere in the room was getting tighter and there was
visible shuffling of bottoms on chairs. I talked a little about Oro
Verdé as a model of good practice, before I moved onto a more
upbeat vision for the British trade:

*I have a vision of a British jewellery sector that is life-affirming.
A collaboration of retailers, manufacturers, and leading jewellery
brands that could bring a significant influence to bear on how
we can be instrumental in improving conditions throughout the
jewellery supply chain. One of the clearest benefits of this would
be to bring a tangible "values added extra" to the British retail/
manufacturer jeweller and introduce a clear USP [Unique Selling
Point] to the British jewellery fashion world. This comes from the
conviction that business is best placed within society to bring about
lasting social change that benefits all the stakeholders within any
given industry. Within our own industry our health, well-being,*

*and future prosperity is dependent upon a diverse and eclectic set of
trading relationships. Many of these relationships do not share in
the prosperity that we do; however, they could do if our industry
embarked upon a courageous journey of enfranchizing the whole
supply chain. This is not beyond our ability.*

*We face some very difficult issues in our industry...
[coupling] this with a more educated consumer who will
increasingly demand more knowledge of product source and
manufacturing conditions, I believe we must respond proactively,
intelligently, and substantially to the social, environmental,
human rights, and livelihoods issue our industry is complicit in.*

*I believe we owe it ourselves, to our suppliers, and most of
all to our customers to offer the finest jewellery created from the
finest materials by the finest designers and supplied from the
finest most life-affirming sources.*

Thank you very much for your time. Any questions?

There was a deep silence in the room as Michael stood up
to facilitate questions. Then an elderly man in the front row
stood up, looked me squarely in the face, and said in the most
condescending and dismissive tone, "Thank you, Mr Valerio, you
can sit down and go away now."

I said nothing. Almost immediately another man rose to his
feet and, in a slightly more worried tone, asked, "Have you spoken
to the press yet?"

I found the response utterly depressing, as these old boys
genuinely did not get it. My reply to the press question was, "Not
yet, but I will be."

All the questions continued in the same manner until
eventually a voice from the back said, "No, these are important
issues and we need to find a way of addressing them as an industry.
The reputation of our industry could be on the line here."

At last, a ray of hope that indicated the message might not be
discounted out of hand by everyone.

The incredulity and cynicism I encountered that day confirmed to me what I had always known; namely that there were large sections of this industry that truly believed that they were impervious to criticism or public perceptions. Had the blood diamond scandal not taught them anything? Clearly a young gun getting up and adding petrol to a fire they were trying to put out was deeply unwelcome. The majority just did not see what human rights and environmental issues had to do with jewellery. There was a pervasive culture of ignoring, avoiding, and suppressing any bad news that might leak out to the consumer.

In fact, it was even worse; all the jewellery in the UK was exploitative of the environment and social labour standards and abusive of human rights in some form or another. There simply was no clean product to be bought on any high street anywhere. But at least there were some individuals who understood what the consequences would be if jewellers did not begin to embrace a more sustainable human rights and environmental agenda. Michael Hoare was one of them, and after the meeting he invited me to a follow-up session to discuss the issues at a later date.

With Christmas trading that year being good, things were now looking up. I had been giving a lot of thought to what ethical jewellery meant and, like most people who desire change, I had been inspired to act out of revulsion for what I had witnessed. The entire debate in my head was being shaped by the negative realities in the trade. What I wanted to create was a more hopeful narrative of what pure jewellery should really look like. I wanted to move away from generic statements like "responsible, sustainable, and ethical" and drill down into the specifics of what these words could mean.

CRED Jewellery had to be the solution. We had to prove the concept that ethical and fair trade jewellery was possible. We now had enough knowledge on the issues to navigate the complexity of the problems, but we still did not have a product that, with hand on heart, I could say was 100 per cent ethical in its creation.

What was now crystal clear to me, as a result of the NRI report, was that transparency and traceability had to be foundational to any claims a jewellery product made to be ethical. Maybe I would learn something in Colombia. I started to dream of a traceable jewellery collection for CRED.

February 2004 saw me struggling with a flu bug as I caught the plane to Colombia. I was completely oblivious to an external world and my throat felt like a world rally championship through an apocalyptic inferno. But even my "man flu" could not dull the excitement I was feeling as I embarked upon my first trip to South America.

Accompanied by Catalina and a few members of a Latin American press entourage, we landed in Quibdó, the departmental capital of the Chocó region on the Pacific coast of Colombia. The Chocó is totally canopied by rainforest, rich in natural minerals such as gold and platinum as well as paramilitaries and guerrillas. These militias use the complex river systems of the Chocó to move their contraband to the ocean. Once there, it could easily be smuggled to the USA. It is a mysterious place full of a beauty, innocence, colour, and tropical promise.

As I stepped off the plane, I breathed in deeply. The air smelt of Africa; that deep earthy smell that lingers in the wind and summons up the primal memory of ancient home. Chocó's main populous are people of African descent, bought by the Spanish as slaves to work the gold mines from the sixteenth century onward. This injustice is the background reality of the Afro-Colombian people and I found the graciousness and dignity they carried toward this horror profoundly moving. Over the course of the ten days I would meet many members of the Afro-Colombian community who, despite being the subject of general Colombian ridicule, were very proud of their African heritage.

In the forest village of Manungara, the community association ASOCASAN (Consejo Comunitario del Alto San Juan, or the Community Council of the Alto San Juan) hosted us, showing the artisanal mining from which their members earned a living. These communities were mining gold using techniques inherited from the ancient Colombian cultures that predated the conquistadors.

The work of the Community Council of the Alto San Juan was remarkable. It was an association formed by thirty villages in the Tado region of Chocó to represent their interests and preserve their way of life. It undertook advocacy work at a regional and national level on land rights and mineral rights issues.

The powerful political and economic interests in the area had led to ongoing conflicts between the rights of small community groups and the vested interests of corporate companies or illegal miners operating as fronts for drug cartels. The little people generally lose. It was here, with the descendants of former slaves and their vibrant communities who extract gold in an environmentally responsible way, that my world was finally opened up to the potential of justice in jewellery.

Ameriko Mosquera's mine was a one-hour drive deeper into the forest along rutted roads running parallel with the biggest river in Chocó, the Rio San Juan. Meeting Ameriko was like meeting a living ebony statue that Michelangelo would have been proud of. Ameriko was in his mid-forties and carved to perfection. A father of eight children, he had clearly been a busy man.

He led us out into the forest through dense undergrowth, still and foreboding with only the sound of running water and what I assumed were large but invisible insects singing to each other to keep us company. We walked for what seemed like miles, following a number of forest streams flowing grey from the silt from mining further upriver. Ameriko explained that this was only temporary. Once the soil stopped being washed, these streams would return to crystal perfection. The ability of the local river courses to clean themselves is one of the ecological indicators that demonstrate that the responsible miners are following sustainable mining practices.

As we climbed up a small watercourse and turned a corner, the landscape opened up in front of us and we entered what seemed like ancient history.

Ameriko's mine had been created out of the devastation of a previous large-scale mining operation some years earlier. It was like walking into a living land sculpture. As the soil was washed, large stones and boulders were exposed, and instead of discarding them, the miners would begin to bank them up in perfect formation, creating large rock terraces reminiscent of an Aztec or Mayan topology. Into this was placed topsoil for preservation that would be used at a later date to start the reforestry programme. Above us was a dammed lake that provided the water for the soil washing. This water cascaded down some thirty feet to the foot of the mine, next to which five members of Ameriko's family were busy cleaning up the mess left by the large-scale miners and removing the remaining gold.

With a large hose powered by a pump, one man sprayed the soil at the base of what can only be described as a slagheap. The soil was washed into the boulder-banked river course and flowed away over three small wooden viaducts that were designed to allow the soil to fall through the grilles to the bottom, thereby catching almost 100 per cent of the gold-rich soil. Then with a traditional round wooden pan the soil was washed in a rhythmic circular motion, eventually leaving the lightest dusting of gold in the middle of the pan.

To watch was to understand the inherent beauty and dignity of work. Ameriko and his family anointed every gram of gold with the dignity of their labour, and were more akin to artists than miners. It was wonderful to see that they did not use mercury to extract the gold: this was the signature of the pioneering ecological approach to mining Oro Verdé had taken. Ameriko could get up to twenty grams of raw gold a day, which was then sold to the not-for-profit marketing company Amichocó for refining and eventual marketing as green gold. I was witnessing the care, the beauty, the artistry, the culture, and creation working in harmony; it was the kind of mining that echoed the romantic images of what a consumer associates with jewellery. I was convinced this was the future for ethical jewellery.

Watching Ameriko and his family working in this way only served to heighten my despair over the motives of large-scale mining companies. I knew they were slaves to the free market dogma of increasing profits at the expense of life itself.

My understanding of the jewellery profession's total reliance on large-scale destruction became more sharply focused and my appreciation grew of why the big jewellery brands wanted to avoid all talk of the source of their products. In one week, a mechanized mining operation could extract as much gold as one small-scale family operation could in two years. This approach to mining destroyed employment opportunities and the sustainability of entire ecosystems. The money then left the region and ended up in shareholders' pockets. It robbed the local people of a sustainable income and displayed the worst possible attitude toward the local culture by leaving these sites as barren wastelands for someone else to clean up.

It was this kind of dirty gold that was ending up on the fingers of newly married people. Ameriko and his family displayed integrity and a care for the environment that allowed me to have fresh hope for the future. I imagined coming back in ten years' time, the forest having completely reclaimed this land, complemented by Ameriko's sculpted mine, and I wondered whether I had discovered one of the ancient secrets of South American culture; harmony with life.

Before leaving the Chocó, we visited the Environmental Research Institute of the Pacific. Its main job is to research and promote environmental sustainability and biodiversity within the Chocó rainforest. They had developed a sophisticated means of determining a healthy ecosystem through a process of identifying indicators that could be taught to the local people and would act as the main criteria for establishing whether a mine was practising ecological sustainability. (In practical terms, this means if you find a certain type of frog in the water, then this is a positive indicator; if you find a certain kind of fungus, then something is going wrong with the mining activity.)

The certifiers spent most of their time in the forest with the miners collecting the bioindicators from wildlife and plant life and teaching the miners to do this job themselves. This process was vital to the whole supply chain. It also acted as the independent certifying body for the sustainable mining practices that Ameriko and the other hundred green gold small-scale mining operations in the Chocó region worked with. The certifying body was always independent of the community associations and other NGOs involved in the process, thereby maintaining the impartiality of the certificates issued to green gold products, and removing any form of conflict of interest that could arise.

Oro Verdé had ploughed a lonely furrow on environmental small-scale mining, arguing that legalizing and empowering small-scale mining communities could have huge long-term benefits for the local ecosystems, long-term job security, the health and education infrastructure of remote communities, as well as bringing much-needed tax revenues to the national exchequer.

Their communitarian approach was working and was better than the religious fervour of Foreign Direct Investment (encouraged by the World Trade Organization, World Bank, and IMF) that created the climate and opportunity for multinational corporate mining companies to exploit resources and move the bulk of the profits to stock markets in foreign countries. This approach destroyed the local communities' opportunities of working the mineral wealth that was under their feet for themselves, took the stewardship of their own ecosystems out of their hands, and placed it in the hands of people who had no understanding of its true worth. The only winners in this kind of system of mining are the minority of people associated with the mining company.

In the city of Medellin, I visited the gold refinery that Oro Verdé used to turn raw gold into refined gold, ready to be used by jewellers. The refining process was perhaps the most boring part of my journey. It was done in a warehouse full of acrid smells and boiling cauldrons, with garish-coloured liquid chemicals in glass jars. The raw gold was placed in a mixed solution of hydrochloric acid and hydrogen peroxide.

Oro Verdé used this refinery because it used hydrogen peroxide instead of nitric acid, a far more damaging and dangerous chemical. Refining gold has to be done chemically, so Oro Verdé chose to work with Señor Gutierrez, as he was the only refiner in Medellin prepared to minimize the chemicals used to refine the gold, and his environmental waste management was very strong. As he said to me, "It pays to be diligent in how we dispose of our waste. Everything we throw away contains a precious metal and precious money."

As I kissed the Chocó goodbye, I knew I had encountered something unique. I had been the first international jeweller to visit their world, eat their food, hear their voices, and share in their lives. The magic was intoxicating and I felt as if the central piece of the jigsaw we had begun to put together in the late nineties had been put into place. I now knew what fair trade ethical jewellery looked like. The challenge was to bring it to market.

Que Pasa Condoto
I watch you
Touching and tasting
The Colombian night
Engrossed in Latin dance
And the release of
Jungle twilight.

She passes love
Like forbidden fruit
And you drink deep
Gulping down sweetness
And breathing in the aphrodisiac
Of sweating muscles
Honed over years of navigating
The warm waters of the Rio Condoto.

Drip your goodness
Over my skin – soak
Me with your heat
So I am drenched
In your hidden lusts
And forbidden treasure.
Paint me green
And delight over me
Teaching me your mysteries
Like an older woman
Instructs the innocence of young men
In wisdom, truth and love.

Que pasa Condoto
I pass into the night
And listen to you sleep.
Be still Condoto
And sleep on the warm breast of God.

CHAPTER FIVE

I will give you the treasures of darkness and riches hidden in secret places.

The prophet Isaiah[1]

Arriving back from Colombia, everything accelerated. I had brazenly placed an order for 100 g of Oro Verdé gold before I left. I was gambling the money we had made the previous Christmas on the wild idea of offering green gold wedding rings. It seemed a marketing "no-brainer" that such a pure source of gold should naturally sit within the wedding jewellery market.

On my first day back in the office, I called Christian and arranged a meeting to brief him on what we required. We needed a new website – www.credjewellery.com – and it needed a luxury feel. We would start with the classic four wedding ring styles. A slightly underwhelming number, admittedly, but they would be the first green gold fully traceable weddings rings in Europe, and very possibly the world, and we would support that with quality photos of the Oro Verdé miners such as Ameriko. We could finally tell the mine-to-market story.

We were about to enter the world of gold jewellery, and despite the excitement, I was also deeply apprehensive. None of us had any experience of working with gold, or the technical challenges around transforming raw gold into a finished product. We had no idea what we were doing. I talked at length to Reuben, the

Chichester store manager, and he confirmed my apprehension, noting our customer base was not at the luxury or bridal end of the market. But he also agreed it was the moral move and we should do it.

The gold arrived six weeks later, rough flakes of pure gold straight from the refinery in Medellin. The challenge we had was: we did not want to contaminate our green gold with any other source of gold. We wanted to guarantee the gold in the ring we sold was the gold that was mined by the Oro Verdé miners. Importantly, we now understood pure gold not only to mean its metallurgical purity, but also its traceable purity, and this meant no contamination.

Here was where we hit problem number one. No manufacturer in the country was remotely interested in batch casting our green gold wedding rings.

"We simply do not handle small isolated batches of gold," was the standard reply. "Try someone else."

None of the UK casting houses was interested in working with us. Poor Christian spent hours on the phone ringing around the country, and every door was shut. Bang, bang, bang, went our heads on the brick wall again.

What we were proposing was so revolutionary in the jewellery world that almost everyone found the concept frightening. "Green gold", "traceability", "ethical provenance", "batch processing", "small amounts", "isolated casting": these phrases were a foreign language to jewellery manufacturers. Our insistence on traceability from mine to retail was exposing the soft ethical underbelly of the entire jewellery manufacturing world. Our battle was not just with the technical challenges our process posed, but also the intellectual, conceptual, and moral challenges around the truth of how jewellery came to market, and its transformation from gold to a finished piece of jewellery.

We discovered an entire worldview change needed to take place before we could even begin to have a conversation with any

UK-based manufacturer on producing our rings, and it was clear their minds were firmly closed. I found it very strange that an industry that predicated itself on the creative and artistic process was very uncreative in how its structures were run. The deeply conservative fraternity that governed the jewellery business had a vested interest in maintaining the status quo.

A hidden truth began to emerge – the luxury jewellery market was built upon a lie, so publicly flaunted that everyone believed it, and so well marketed that no one could see through the smokescreen to get to the truth. The public marketing face of jewellery was seductive, feminine, expensive, and aspirational, intentionally divorcing the finished product from the source that was dirty, masculine, abusive, violent, and a monopolistic untraceable and untransparent practice, its wealth consolidated in the hands of the few. Given the real truth of jewellery, the luxury brands had to spend billions a year maintaining the illusion of the purity of their product to prop up their value.

This campaign was so effective that consumers simply did not connect jewellery to mining in the same way that they connected their trainers to sweat shops or their food to a free-range source. However, CRED now had a clean, traceable source of gold from ecologically beautiful mines, a refiner who kept the metal separate, and full traceability from mine to retail. But how would we turn this gold into a wedding ring?

I received an invitation to attend the Jewellers Christian Fellowship in London. I had no idea such a thing existed, but agreed to go. The very earnest attendees supped white wine in the sumptuous surroundings of the Sloane Street Boodles jewellery store, and they listened very attentively to my stories of India, Colombia, poverty in mining, and the environmental destruction associated with our business. I vented my growing frustrations with the UK manufacturing intelligence deficit on batch casting, and wrapped my stories up in God's priority for the poor and commitment to creation.

For some attendees it was clearly a heretical message; for others, very compelling. My intention was to fashion a moral, social, and environmental purpose that could underpin our reason, as Christians, for being in the jewellery trade, other than perpetuating the luxury mythology and lining our pockets at the expense of the poor.

Brian Fulton, a jeweller from Cumbria, offered to help us out. He was a goldsmith and was fascinated by the idea of an ethical purity being possible in jewellery. Brian would prove to be a Godsend in the early days, as his twenty years of experience in the profession plugged the skills gap we had on the team.

Having explained the need for full traceability to be maintained on our wedding ring offer, he said he would hand-make our wedding rings on his jewellery bench in his studio in the Lake District. This was perfect for us. We now had provenance on our gold source, and had a goldsmith hand-making our rings here in the UK. My headache was starting to heal.

In May 2004, CRED Jewellery launched the world's first dedicated ethical jewellery website, selling green gold wedding rings. We offered four simple classic styles of wedding ring; the court, the flat court, the D-shaped and the flat band. We kept our offer to 18 ct yellow and white gold only and we waited. We would have loved to have been able to do more, but very simply we did not have the money to do anything but the basics.

Almost immediately we began to get customers. They would tell us they really loved the idea of environmental green gold, and why had no one done this before? What was apparent in almost all of our feedback was that people had just never made the direct link between jewellery and the mineral extraction industries, never mind having any knowledge of small-scale miners. They thanked us that we had joined the dots and allowed them to look back to the source of their gold. It was obvious that people felt embarrassed to admit they had never thought about the source of their jewellery before.

To start with, we were serving two to three customers a month and this continued to grow. It also meant our orders for green gold began to grow and soon we were buying 250 g a time. I was also beginning to get regular interest from local and industry press, following on from the NAG presentation. Most of it was not that complimentary, but at least it was now overt rather than in the shadows as it had been before. People would ask me how I felt about the rumour mill calling me all kinds of names. I was actually quite happy, as it was giving us more press and publicity than we had ever had. If you don't have enemies, how can the battle for progress be defined?

We were featured in the local Chichester Observer that Christmas. I talked about Colombia, traceable green gold, the social and environmental devastation of large-scale mining, and how the jewellery trade was linked to this. I encouraged customers to start asking difficult questions when they bought jewellery, and explained how our wedding rings represented the best in the industry, as they were non-exploitative.

Then The Goldsmith Magazine published an article on ethical jewellery, attacking the claims we were making and saying it was impossible for us to do traceable gold. They had got their information from a local jeweller who was deeply upset with us and complained we were impugning his business integrity by making claims about the ethical value of our rings. He had begun to ring up the trade associations and magazines, attempting to get negative press placed wherever possible. But again I took this as a positive sign: we at last were being taken seriously. I found it deeply ironic that established jewellers and elements of the trade press seemed to be so threatened by a little south coast jeweller doing about a dozen green gold wedding rings a month.

In the middle of the excitement and interest in our launch of green gold wedding rings, Catalina called me from Colombia to ask if I would attend a round table conference in Quito, Ecuador. For some time she had been dreaming of starting a South

American association of small-scale miners that could build on the experiences of Oro Verdé. She wanted me to come over as a jeweller and talk to the miners about the principles of fair trade and our experiences of working with Oro Verdé. We both recognized the simple power of miners and jewellers meeting, sharing experiences and doing business.

Arriving in Quito, I was picked up and taken to the guesthouse where we would spend the next three days in discussions about the proposal. Around the table were a number of experts in small-scale mining, funding agencies from the Netherlands, cultural anthropologists, and small-scale miners from Argentina, Colombia, Peru, Ecuador, Bolivia, and Enki, the beer-trading Mongolian part-time gold miner, who seemed more focused on selling crates of his beer than he was on the purpose of the meeting. And so began my four-year relationship with what would become the Alliance for Responsible Mining (ARM).

It was a difficult three days for me, sitting in a small dark room, listening to Spanish dialogue through a translator, with endless PowerPoint presentations to back it up, and thick black coffee, cigarettes, and Enki's beer. The debates on what this association could look like went on for hours and into a level of detail I found extremely hard to follow, due to the language difficulties. This was not the trip of adventure, exploration, and discovery that I had grown accustomed to. This was a process meeting, a construct meeting, a detail and planning meeting.

But it was also a meeting that (however difficult I found it to concentrate) proved to be seminal when I reflected on it with the luxury of hindsight. It was a meeting for miners, and I felt privileged to have been invited. I was moved by the struggles of the small-scale miners to get political recognition for their livelihoods, and the clarity of their cause helped me to get through the waves of boredom that often settled on me.

These miners talked about the formalization of artisanal and small-scale mining, and how their governments refused to recognize that the work they did was a legitimate business opportunity. They described how they were constantly marginalized by government policy that only reflected the requirements and needs of the big mining companies, and how their governments were constantly in the pockets of these companies. Their community and ancestral lands were often taken away from them without their prior consent or consultation, and given to large mining companies from other countries, all because there was gold under the villages.

These men were very proud of their work. They were miners, and this was embedded into their identity. The struggle to be recognized as men was etched on their faces and echoed in the tone of their voices. There was real dignity and honour in being a miner and, as I sat listening, my mind wandered back to the miners' strike in Britain in the mid eighties. I could hear the same fight for recognition and identity in the voices of our own UK mining industry. I began to understand in a more profound way why the destruction of the mining industry by Margaret Thatcher's government had been such a cataclysmic event in British history. She had not just dismantled an industry, she had destroyed the soul of those communities, committing a crime against humanity, and Britain still lives with that legacy today.

These small-scale miners had faced huge challenges in organizing their communities to fight these injustices and to lobby their own governments to get their small-scale approach to mining written into the mineral laws of their respective countries. So the proposal to form an alliance to represent small-scale miners was an exciting development for them, as working together across the countries they represented meant they would make a louder and more effective noise.

When it came to my turn, I dispensed with the PowerPoint-less presentation and decided to tell my story as an ethical jeweller: my journeys in India, Nepal, and Colombia, and how as a jeweller I was seeking to respond to some of the injustices in the mining sector, through delivering mine to market traceability with Oro Verdé. By connecting that struggle for justice to the customers of my jewellery, I would tell the story of the miners and their environment. I also talked at length about fair trade and its principles of being a commercial framework that sought to put the marginalized and the poor at the heart of the business transaction. Fair trade equals economic justice for the poor, I explained, and there is no reason why we could not do this in gold as it had already been done in tea, coffee, and bananas.

For the miners this was a very new idea, but one they thought was good. They also began to see where their gold ended up. I learned that traceability was as important to the miners as it was to me as a jeweller. Despite our cultural, economic, linguistic, and national differences, we all wanted the same thing: transparency and traceability in the supply chain.

On the last day, it was decided to form an association. And so it came to the vote for who would be the founding board members. There was lots of discussion about process and procedure, all in Spanish, and by now cabin fever was setting in.

Toward what I hoped would be the end of the discussion, I left the room to go to the toilet and have a cigarette, my mind numb with boredom. When I returned, I found my name written down as a nominee for the inaugural board. Voting started, and by the end of the vote I had become a founding board member of the Alliance for Responsible Mining. My relationship with ARM would become a defining moment in the creation of what would become certified Fairtrade and Fairmined gold, but for now we closed the meeting by appointing an interim manager, who was charged with drafting the vision and mission for ARM. We would reconvene in six months' time in Lima to vote the constitution of ARM into place. The making of history in mining and jewellery had taken a significant step forward.

Back at home, my relationship with the National Association of Goldsmiths was developing well. I had met Michael Hoare a few times now and I really liked him. I respected his English practicality. Since my infamous presentation earlier the previous year, I had been giving some thought to establishing an Ethical Jewellery Initiative in the UK and had finally got round to putting some thoughts down on paper.

We met to discuss the idea and I proposed we set this up inside the NAG and mirror the principles of the Ethical Trading Initiative as closely as possible. I was not interested in starting another organization for the sake of it. We could establish the initiative around the bedrock principles of transparency and traceability and, building on that foundation, look at each section of the industry, product by product, and map the supply chains. It would also set a framework of ethical conduct for manufacturers. I thought it was a great idea, but I could see a deep strain of pragmatism appear on his face as I explained it. He knew that the UK industry was not ready for such a discussion.

At one of our meetings, he invited a representative of Jewelers of America into our discussion. Michael was keen for us to meet. Apparently the representative was busy shaping a similar idea for the corporate sector of the jewellery industry.

There is something slightly surreal about corporate America. I liken it to walking into the world of Barbie and Ken. It looks a little like real life, but it lacks soul and is devoid of individual personality. The only thing that animates the corporate spirit is the power of money. It is precisely this vacuum of individuality and personality and its insistence on a one-size-fits-all model that has always made me feel uncomfortable and wary when in its presence.

The representative was a nice guy, but he was corporate America and had the suit to prove it; non-descript. Michael wanted him to hear about my idea and I gave an outline of what a responsible jewellery industry could look like. The representative was thinking along the same lines and wanted to establish a council for responsible jewellery practice, bring together all the key stakeholders in the jewellery supply chain, and work on setting standards for each section, such as refiners, cutters and polishers, mining companies, and retailers. This was of course a very good idea, but it was clear he was only thinking of the big players in the industry: the gold and diamond mining companies and corporate luxury brands such as Cartier and Tiffany.

As I listened, it became increasingly obvious that the small jewellers and small-scale miners were not a part of the plan. He naturally disputed this, claiming that the leading national trade association would be the representatives of the small jewellers, but to my ears that sounded political rather than deliverable.

Michael was honest with me after the meeting that the NAG would be supporting this process as it was politically expedient to do so, and couldn't see where my ideas could fit in. However, I was not too despondent; at least there was some form of movement within the industry to begin to address ethical issues, even if my personal view was the Council for Responsible Jewellery Practice would become a big boys' top-down one-size-fits-all refuge for those wanting to avoid negative publicity about their ethical performance.

It was extraordinary to think that within a year of each other, ARM (a bottom-up approach to community mining and empowerment) and CRJP (a top-down Corporate Social Responsibility initiative) had both started. It was a further clarifying of the future choices the jewellery industry would be presented with.

That summer, I was invited to speak at the Eden Project. This iconic ecological project, built out of an old abandoned mine in Cornwall, would be a symbolic location in which to speak about ethical jewellery and ecological gold mining. The Association for Contemporary Jewellers had picked up the vibration in the industry surrounding the ethical provenance of the materials being used by jewellers and wanted to hear the CRED story.

At the end of my talk, I was inundated with attendees all agreeing with the simple proposition that traceability in the supply side of jewellery was a very serious issue that needed to be addressed. This became the spark that started the fire burning amongst the small bench jewellers who mostly work from home or in small studios. It appeared that I was not the only small jeweller who cared: actually there were hundreds of us. Very soon my inbox was filled up with jewellers wanting to know more about how to do it.

Vivien Johnston was the first jeweller to ring me. A slip of a Scot, she was working for a well-known Scottish jewellery brand as a quality controller and designer. Her job entailed visiting factories in the Far East that the company used to manufacturer their collections. What she witnessed had led her to seriously question the working conditions and labour standards, and her conscience was prompting her to set up her own ethical jewellery company. April Doubleday was an artisan designer–maker based in Devon, and had been at the Eden Project presentation. Like Vivien, she was shocked at the human rights abuses in jewellery and was looking for a cleaner way of delivering her collections.

The trickle continued. David Rhode of Ingle & Rhode came for lunch, trying to work out how we were doing it. Jos Skeates, the owner and founder of EC One Jewellery, became another jeweller to invite me to talk to him and his staff about the ethical issues we all faced in the industry. Diana Porter rang asking for info and help on how to visit the miners in Colombia. And so it continued: every week the office would get calls from jewellers around the country wanting to know more. These jewellers were passionate about the issues and wanted to take practical steps to improve their ethical performance.

Others, however, were more cynical in their approach. They recognized that the emerging national discussion around ethics was likely to become a future trend, and they, like most of the industry, did not have a clue how to deliver the emerging idea of traceability. CRED was ahead of the curve and so some calls could be more about stealing our ideas and contacts than about genuinely caring for the conditions of workers or the state of the environment. It became increasingly apparent that we would not be the only jeweller doing ethical jewellery for very much longer.

All these conversations sparked a major discussion within CRED. We had created a considerable amount of know-how around our business process as jewellers. We had a good international network of suppliers, refiners, and manufacturers who helped us to deliver 100 per cent traceable jewellery from mine to market. We could make our process proprietorial and keep it secret, the normal convention in the jewellery trade, or we could be open-handed, recognizing that what we were doing was motivated by a higher authority than simply profit, securing our economic advantage and ultimately excluding others.

It was a huge dilemma for me. The perceived wisdom in business is to protect your advantage; protect your bottom line financial advantage, make it as difficult as possible for others to follow you – and maintain your commercial advantage at all costs. Ruth and I had invested all our life savings, remortgaged the house twice, and I had gone without a salary for long periods of time, to prove that fair trade jewellery was possible. We had the most to lose if we chose to be open-handed. What would happen if another company stole our ideas and did a better job because they had more money than us?

This was one of the most difficult tests I faced. I had broken through the industry cynicism and belief that fair trade traceable jewellery was impossible. We were now delivering a green gold wedding ring that proved traceability in the supply chain was possible. It was now apparent that there was a fledgling movement of small jewellers who wanted to do the same, and to coalesce around a human rights and environmental justice agenda.

I spent a number of days praying and not eating about this. I was tested as to my motives, my ego, my desire for wealth and comfort and personal security. I was reminded of my belief that all of creation is a gift from God, and private ownership is the ultimate illusion, as you can take nothing with you in death. I remembered that the resources of the land such as gold and diamonds are there to benefit the people of the land and bring wealth and prosperity to the poor. I began to understand that transparency and traceability were not just socio-political concepts and constructs to be applied to supply chains but are, in spiritual language, those ancient essential realities of truth and light. Light (transparency) does not change anything; it merely reveals what exists, so everyone can see clearly its true nature. Truth (traceability) was the medium through which the corruptions of the industry could be put right, and customers could buy a product that was pure and contained an essential veracity of honesty and justice.

Ultimately you cannot serve God and Mammon, and jewellery was a confused mixture of the two. On one hand, it was a deeply corrupt product because it lied to people about its origins, but it was also a talisman of aspiration, love, beauty, and creativity. Given these undeniable convictions, we decided to move forward in an open-handed way, and give away what we had learned, in the hope that it would spawn a movement nationally and internationally that would deliver justice through jewellery.

We knew what the implications of this would be, but it was the only moral course of action open to us. If we did not act with an open hand, we would end up becoming the very thing we were standing against: a corrupt, self-serving company that would get rich on the back of the poor. After all, a pound of truth is worth a million pounds of PR, and we did not have a million pounds.

CHAPTER SIX

I sit on a man's back choking him and making him carry me, and yet assure myself and others that I am sorry for him and wish to lighten his load by all means possible... except by getting off his back.

Leo Tolstoy

By the autumn of 2004, CRED was now facing an unforeseen problem. We had gone out on a limb with green gold and proved the concept, but now our customers started asking us for ethical fair trade diamonds. Having gained the reputation of being a fair trade ethical jeweller, it was a logical progression for us. The challenge was: I knew very little about diamonds. The only diamonds we sold were the small pave diamonds that were set into silver by Hot Diamonds, at the time one of Britain's most popular silver jewellery brands. These stones were typically 1 mm or 2 mm wide and did not have any serious financial value. A stone for an engagement ring was another proposition altogether. We had set the bar quite high on ethical performance, and as we began to apply the same due diligences to the diamond trade, we began to see that to repeat the same ethical proposition in diamonds would be a mountain even bigger than gold.

We wanted diamonds that were transparent, traceable, conflict-free, and from the hand of the artisanal miners. Where could we find such a stone? I was now becoming known as a fair trade jeweller and was beginning to think I had set myself an impossible task. Having spent years in search of pure gold, my customers (and let us not forget they are the ones who are always right) had decided they wanted a fair trade diamond that would match the ethical credentials of the Oro Verdé gold we had been using. But I was unaware of where to go looking for such a thing. Instinctively I felt this would be an almost impossible task.

Sixty per cent of all the rough diamonds in the world at the time were mined by the De Beers Group, and they remain the biggest and most influential player in the diamond trade. Yet, by their own confession, their diamonds were not fair trade, as the value these sales created did not directly go to the poor or marginalized diamond miners. Therefore, securing a diamond that was mined according to a set of fair trade principles was going to be a great challenge.

In a conversation with Susie Sanders from Global Witness at the beginning of 2005, I discussed the challenge of finding such a diamond. I explained I was looking for a diamond that reflected the values of peace, shared prosperity, and community participation that in all its classical simplicity would break the rules and offer a fairer cut to the alluvial diamond digger. Susie recommended I attend the Peace Diamond Alliance Conference in Sierra Leone.

The Peace Diamond Alliance (PDA) had been established at the heart of the Kono district in eastern Sierra Leone in 2002. Sierra Leone had become synonymous with the words "blood diamonds" as the recent bloody civil war had been funded from the diamond fields of this small West African country. He who controlled the diamonds controlled the country, and the Kono district was in the middle of this conflict. So I booked myself into their conference and headed out to post-war Sierra Leone, hoping to find an answer to my fair trade diamond question.

The six-hour journey east into the heart of Sierra Leone was better than I expected it to be. We travelled past endless rice paddies, hectic little African roadside towns, police checkpoints, and UN vehicles scuttling up the road with an air of great importance. I knew we were getting close to Koidu Town, the heart of the diamond mining area, when I began to see the telltale signs of small-scale mining activity. Patches of land were heavily deforested, piles of earth scattered around as though some monstrous demonic mole had been ripping the land up. There were pools of water the size of big fish ponds in which men, stripped down to their waists, with picks and shovels, were busy tearing up the soil and sifting through the dirt as though their lives depended on it, which of course they did.

Visiting the alluvial diamond fields of Sierra Leone was in most ways no different to visiting any other small-scale mining activity, but it had one added difference. Here you had the added exhilaration of the casino. Every digger – of whom there were thousands – believed he was going to be the man who found the big one, the big stone that would make him a millionaire. But, like all casinos, the odds were heavily stacked against him. The diamond-rich ground of Kono has been continually mined over the last thirty years and the big diamond finds have all but disappeared. Yet in this fragile world of grinding poverty and vain hope, sheer desperation drove the diggers to live the sorcerous existence of the addicted gambler. The diamond has cast its spell and everyone in Koidu has come under its influence. This began to include our own party.

As we walked in the heat of day around the diamond pits, I began to notice behaviour changes in the group of academics, businessmen, and consultants who were also attending the PDA's annual conference. The casino fervour was clearly having an effect on them. As I looked back over my shoulder, I saw fully grown men scrabbling around in the diamond tailings, picking up small rocks, praying one would be a diamond. Diamonds were obviously warping rational minds into patterns of strange behaviour.

As we negotiated our way through the random pits of stagnant water and tailings piles, I saw a group of women emerge from the scrubland with children strapped to their backs and washing pans under their arms. They waded into one of the washing pits, hitched their skirts up to their hips and began washing out the soils under their feet. What were they doing? Clearly they were not washing for diamonds, as they did not have the distinctive grilled washing pans normally associated with sorting rough diamond.

I began talking to them. The women explained that every day, around three in the afternoon, they would come down while the diamond diggers were on their break and pan for gold. In just a few hours they could wash around 1 g of gold, which they would then sell to a local trader for 3,000 leones. This equalled about $1.50 per woman for two to three hours' work. This was good money for them and acted as a regular income that paid the rent and food bills on a daily basis. When I asked them why they were not looking for diamonds, their reply was a typically pragmatic one. "Diamonds are a fool's game that only men play. There are not enough diamonds to feed our children. Gold is our daily bread."

In the conference itself, people soon became aware of the work I was doing with CRED, Oro Verdé, and ARM, and the early successes we were having in building a transparent gold supply chain. Although I was only there as an observer, they asked me to contribute my story and experiences in a plenary session and also to help lead a workshop with the miners who were interested in gold. As I sat in the workshop group of about thirty men and women, we were tasked to explore the relationship between gold and diamonds.

"How many here mine diamonds?" I asked. All the men in the group put up their hands. "How many mine gold?" All the women put up their hands, and only one man. My next question focused on the money. "How much do diamond diggers earn per day?"

"One dollar plus a cup full of rice," they replied. The men also explained that if they found a stone of significant value, they would be entitled to a share from the proceeds of the sale. When asked how many men had found a diamond of any real value in the last six months, they all confessed they had not.

When the women were asked the same question, they were all earning around $10 a week from panning gold. This was far more than the men were earning, and all for a fraction of the backbreaking work. I did not understand why more of the men were not panning for gold, so I asked them.

"It is women's work!" came the chorus from the men. "Women do gold, men do the diamonds, and one day we will find the big stone and get rich. You'll never get rich mining gold."

The bewitching power of alluvial diamond digging was fully exposed. "How many of you have become rich from mining diamonds?" I asked. Not one man answered the question; clearly there was now a level of embarrassment surrounding the earlier displays of hubris.

The women had sat very quietly throughout the posturing. I learned from them that all the money they earned went straight into feeding the family, whereas the money the men earned was more often than not spent with the local beer seller. I closed our workshop having seen a small glimpse into the lives and mindsets of diamond miners.

"Who is the more intelligent miner?" I asked. "The man who works four times as hard for half the money, or the woman who pays the rent and feeds the family and earns twice as much for a fraction of the work?" The women roared with laughter at the prospect of being declared more intelligent than men, but the facts were irrefutable.

The Peace Diamond Alliance was attempting to bring some order into this lottery of madness. The challenge was defined by the PDA very succinctly.

To sustain the hard won peace Sierra Leone must address
the fundamental problems that led to and sustained the war.

Central among them is the issues of mismanagement of the diamond resource and the related lack of transparency and environmental degradation.

One of the biggest issues central to the integrity of the diamond mining activities in Sierra Leone was the problem of smuggling. This in turn was having a massive impact on the international diamond trade. Rough diamond was being smuggled out of the country and finding its way to the international bourses and the cutting and polishing centres around the world, such as Antwerp and Surat in India, where it became untraceable. This was tainting the entire market and consumer confidence in the diamond product.

This diamond smuggling was big business, fuelled corruption, lined the pockets of racketeers, and denied the government essential revenues for rebuilding the country. Jewellers like me who wished to see diamonds bring real benefits to poorer countries like Sierra Leone were insisting on a Kimberley Process that guaranteed the diamond they bought was certified conflict-free from mine to retail.

The obvious weakness of the Kimberley Process (KP) was that it only covered rough diamonds that would be exported or imported from one country to another; it is essentially a customs procedure governed by the member states that had signed up to the Kimberley protocols. What it did not do was guarantee to the consumer that any cut and polished stone that ended up in an engagement ring would be conflict-free, not smuggled or corrupt, as illicit rough stone could be mixed into parcels of legitimate stones and then exported under a KP certificate and be called "conflict-free". Essentially it could not act as a guarantee for the consumer, despite the fact that jewellers were using the KP as a consumer guarantee when they were selling diamonds.

To reinforce the fact, I had a chance evening meal in Freetown with a Namibian I met in the bar of the hotel I was staying at.

He was unapologetic and very open about consulting for the Russian mafia on the diamond system in Sierra Leone. He told me that thousands of carats of stones were being smuggled out of the country into Russia, mixed with Russian production, and exported out of Russia under the Kimberley certificates.

The PDA, in order to counter this corruption, had set itself the task of developing a transparent, fair, and safe local market. They were trying to maximize the benefits to local miners, diggers, and their communities by introducing systems to track the rough diamond from the mine to export through mobilizing local surveillance at the mine site. This would minimize smuggling and corruption, and hopefully restore confidence in the system as a whole. A diamond from the PDA would be a clean diamond and represent the start of something we all hoped would catch on around the country, if not the world.

They also had an impressive range of other activities such as funding credit schemes for miners, buying diamonds that were certified by the Alliance to be branded and sold as "peace diamonds", procuring transportation and communications equipment for the ministry of mineral resources, training miners and diggers on the value of their production, addressing issues of child labour, educating the local community on developing alternatives to diamond mining, and continuing to strengthen the local institutions so they were more democratic and representative of the community. All this was being funded by the United States Agency for International Development (USAID), the UK's Department for International Development, and De Beers, who were adding expertise to ensure that the process was a long-term success.

However, this was only the beginning for the PDA. To build upon the excellent work they had done in the previous two years in transforming the horror of the blood diamond story to one of peace and potential prosperity, they would require a number of factors to emerge that were beyond their control.

First, the Sierra Leone government had to drastically improve their management of the diamond sector and put more resources into counter-smuggling activities. Secondly, the country must remain peaceful. It was a tragic reality that almost everyone I spoke to expected the conflict to return at some point in the future and were desperate that the international community continue to follow through on their commitment not to abandon Sierra Leone. Thirdly, the issue of land reform needed to be addressed, allowing miners rights and privileges over their own means of production. The system was run by what amounted to a feudal structure where patrimonial chiefs exercised total control over who did what and who would benefit from the diamonds that were found. One of the major beneficiaries of the current system was, surprisingly, the tribal chiefs.

With some of the mountain conquered, the PDA had risen to the challenge and was starting the journey toward developing a peace diamond. Perhaps the most significant contribution that the PDA had made to date was being prepared to swim against the tide by planting a flag in the ground around which the local communities, private investors, governments, jewellery businesses, and civil society groups could rally.

However, the PDA required the public to rise above the exquisitely polished rhetoric surrounding diamonds and to insist that the jewellery trade provide fairly traded traceable diamonds that offered peace and prosperity for everyone in the diamond supply chain. With a diamond that sought the common good for all humanity, we could make this icon of beauty free from any hint of exploitation and corruption. For these reasons a peace diamond was essential and might contribute to the rewriting of the tedious script that diamonds only benefit the large-scale diamond mining companies, the wealthy, and the beautiful.

On my journey in Sierra Leone it became apparent that the PDA was a long way from securing its goal, never mind me fulfilling my personal aspiration of being able to purchase a peace diamond.

However, an unexpected outcome of the trip was meeting Simon Gilbert, who worked for De Beers in London in their external affairs department.

Simon had spent nearly twenty years with De Beers as a buyer in the Democratic Republic of the Congo and had a wealth of expertise on the alluvial diamond issues we had been exploring with the PDA. Listening to Simon on the complexities of the diamond supply chain made me realize how little I actually knew about this specific side of the jewellery trade, despite my previous experiences in gemstones and gold. Although we disagreed on whether a fair trade diamond was feasible or desirable, given the political complexities of the diamond and the highly stylized marketing narrative written to maintain its luxury value, he was incredibly helpful.

We sat in the courtyard of our little Koidu hostel, drinking beer and drawing diagrams on the back of envelopes of what the small-scale miners' diamond supply chain looked like. From the digger, the stone travelled through the hands of a myriad of "comptoirs" or traders and was consolidated with lots of other diamonds from similar locations. From here it was most likely to be smuggled out of Sierra Leone to the diamond-trading bourses in Israel, Antwerp, India, or New York to be sold as rough diamond parcels that then would be cut and polished for the jewellery trade. The person who put the most work into the system was the miner, who in the majority of cases was paid $1 and a cup of rice for his twelve hours of daily labour.

I almost fell off my bar stool when Simon offered to arrange a time for me to sit in on the internal De Beers diamond graders training at their Charterhouse Street HQ in London. It was a very generous offer. My trip to Sierra Leone had been amazingly educational, but I had failed to achieve my primary purpose of securing a traceable diamond. Clearly we were not going to get a stone from the hands of an African alluvial diamond miner in the near future, so we needed to look around for alternative sources.

The political landscape of the jewellery world was heating up intensively by September 2005. I received an invitation (via Simon Gilbert) to attend the non-profit consultation day that the Responsible Jewellery Council (RJC) was hosting at the Radisson Hotel in Antwerp. The contrast between the poverty-riddled diamond pits of Sierra Leone and the opulence of the jewellery power brokers could not have been more extreme. I had known an organization of some sorts was going to emerge, mainly from my earlier conversations with Michael Hoare of NAG and the representative of Jewelers of America, but had heard nothing else about it until now. As with all corporate affairs, it was an extremely well-hosted event designed to woo the NGOs and campaign group invitees who were assembled from around the world.

As I sat down next to Michael Rae from World Wildlife Fund (WWF) Australia, the gathering that was assembled in the grand ballroom genuinely impressed me. Human Rights Watch, the WWF, Global Witness, the Catholic Agency For Overseas Development (CAFOD), Earthworks, and many others were all there to listen to what the jewellery industry was going to do to sort itself out. Many of these groups, such as Global Witness, Human Rights Watch, and Earthworks, had a long track record of criticizing large-scale mining companies and jewellery brands over their poor track record on human and indigenous rights and the considerable environmental damage and pollution they caused. The had also launched campaigns like No Dirty Gold and Unearth Justice, focusing on the jewellers' role in perpetuating the damage being done by extraction industries.

The background to RJC went way back to the late nineties, when the diamond industry was discovered to be powerless to stop the flow of blood diamonds entering into the world market from countries such as Sierra Leone, Angola, and the Democratic Republic of the Congo. De Beers, caught in the maelstrom of negative public opinion about diamonds and the obvious threat this created to the consumer perceptions about the value of the stones, moved to quell the storm by a radical shake-up in the political governance of the jewellery world.

The impact of blood diamonds was two-fold. First, the diamond fields where the fighting and exploitation was occurring created real horror and misery for ordinary poor people. Secondly, the jewellery trade was being scandalized. Up until then, the diamond trade had been printing money off the backs of this misery. The negative international publicity prompted the industry to speak of its moral outrage and take action. In the face of the inability of the international diamond manufacturers and the international diamond bourses, and traders, to stop the flow of blood diamonds entering the world market, De Beers had told them they were useless, and that they were going to set up another body called the World Diamond Council (WDC), who would be given a mandate to govern what would become the Kimberley Process. The existing diamond operators would all be able to contribute to the WDC, but effectively would do what they were told in regards to blood diamonds. It was stark reminder to everyone in the industry who really wields the power in jewellery; namely, the mining companies. Naturally this kind of power wielded by De Beers created resentments that would surface later. So as I walked into the room in Antwerp, I was totally unaware of the geo-politics in jewellery that was outworking itself before my eyes.

At the top table sat the Corporate Responsibility directors of Rio Tinto, De Beers, Jewelers of America, and some of the A-list jewellery brands such as Tiffany and Cartier. The RJC was being called into position to protect the integrity of the gold and diamond supply chain.

To understand the significance of this, you have to understand how the jewellery trade works. The diamond is the key to the value of the jewellery industry. It is what carries the real value in every significant jewellery sale, and the romance of the stone carries the purity of the brand value across the entire sector. Basically, you don't mess with the diamond story: to do so would expose the soft underbelly in the industry. There was no way De Beers and others were going to let the perceived value of diamonds be eroded in the consumer mind through allowing the hard-won perception of the purity of diamonds to be associated with war and conflicts.

So, with the help of Rio Tinto, another big diamond miner based out of Australia, and the representative from Jewelers of America, they had set about establishing the RJC. Matt Runci was critical to the delivery of RJC as he represented the world's biggest market for retail diamond jewellery, America.

The stage was set for a full day's entertainment as the objectives of this new fledgling trade association were presented to the world and its detractors. It was clear from the outset that my suspicions about the RJC, stemming from my first meeting with the representative from Jewelers of America at the NAG, proved correct. RJC was not an inclusive set-up. Its principal protagonists all came from the corporate mining sector and big jewellery brands. They wanted to create standards that could be applied to large corporate members who were the principal recipients of the profits to be made in the diamond and gold supply chain.

The idea was to be able to certify each operator in the jewellery supply chain, such as mining operations, refiners, jewellery companies, diamond cutting and polishing houses, and all the other actors that fed into the big money chain. What they were not going to do was certify the actual products that went through the hands of their potential members.

This disconnect between operators and the goods they handled was a big gap in the proposal. Effectively a RJC council member could handle smuggled diamonds or dirty gold and they would still be certified as responsible, because the word "responsible" was only to be applied to how they ran their factory or manufacturing unit. The RJC were not going to tackle the real issue of traceability in the supply chain of the gold or diamonds.

It smelled of corporate green wash, and it was Michael Rae of the WWF that led the NGO charge by highlighting the impact of large-scale operations in Australia and the negative impact mining had on the surrounding ecosystems. If the RJC were going to do anything of substance, it would have to be fully transparent to gain the acceptance of the civil society groups at the table.

I made it very clear at the meeting that in real terms this body did not represent the majority of the jewellery trade. It represented the big boys, and if they were very serious about cleaning up the supply chain and genuinely tackling the root causes of conflict minerals, smuggled goods, and corruption, then they must include small-scale miners in the decision-making process. Also, it was all very well having Tiffany and Cartier and other luxury brands being covered by the RJC, but they did not represent the overriding majority in our industry. What was needed was an organization that included everyone, including the campaign groups; an organization in which we could all work together in an inclusive framework, not a corporate one that left the small jewellers and miners out in the cold. What was being proposed was a consolidation of the same power base with a different name; a rearranging of the deckchairs.

And so the discussion went on. Everyone in the room was basically saying the same thing – more inclusivity: an organization where power was shared by all the different-sized operators in the industry and a supply chain that was transparent. However, these things were never going to happen, as the diamond companies and luxury jewellery brands were never going to give away control of the market share or the brand value attached to it into the hands of the industry's great unwashed. They wanted to make sure they had established a system that would serve their purposes before they allowed other smaller operators inside the club.

The long speeches and the endless jargon emanating from the top table, whose aim seemed to be to fill the room with noise and cover up the shortfalls in the RJC construct, were boring me. In establishing RJC, greater fractures emerged in the jewellery world, as The World Federation of Jewellers (CIBJO) pulled their support from RJC on the grounds that the RJC was an elitist organisation that did not and could not represent the rank and file of the jewellery industry. RJC, in trying to do the right thing, seemed to be falling between a rock and a hard place.

I had been invited, according to Simon Gilbert, because what we had done with Oro Verdé meant we were ahead of the curve on ethical issues as we had genuine traceability in our supply chain, something none of the others brands had at the time. Simon had invited me in to shake up the discussion and demonstrate to the big players what was achievable, if you had the political will to walk the walk.

I was beginning to get a clearer idea of the impact our little company was having on the industry as a whole, and also how fractured and dirty the politics in the jewellery industry really was.

The meeting finished in the usual way, with disgruntled NGOs and campaign groups talking of fudge and green wash and the industry saying it was just the beginning – trust us and please come back in a year and judge our progress. But the most illuminating outcome of the day was that within a matter of months, Michael Rae, the most vocal detractor in the room, was appointed as the CEO of the RJC. I did rather mischievously wonder whether the whole day had been a big en-masse job interview.

Back at home, my three days of training with De Beers came around very quickly. As I walked through the security doors I was greeted very warmly, and the diamond trainer led me upstairs to their training floor. I tried to look very casual and nonplussed as I encountered tables of rough diamonds laid out in meticulous fashion with signs indicating their origin of denomination. There were diamond parcels from Russia, Namibia, Canada, Botswana, and South Africa.

It was the colour differences I noticed instantly. Namibian stones had the purest intense white colour and, as the diamonds cascaded through my hands like water, I could not help but remind my conscience of why I was in this industry. Here I was holding a million pounds-worth of stones in my hand, while miners in Sierra Leone were lucky to earn a dollar a day. Here I was in the bowels of the iconoclastic keeper of the diamond story, when only a few months previously I had been knee-deep in the mud of Sierra Leone with women and children digging for diamonds and gold. The moral contrast was deeply disturbing.

The small group on the training were led on a tour of the numerous floors of the buildings, all of which focused on sorting and grading different carat weights of diamond. The smallest stones were sorted in machines specifically designed to move volume. Buckets of small diamonds would be poured in to the top of the machine and they would cascade down through the machine like some kind of millionaire mathematical conundrum, eventually being sorted into size grades in smaller trays ready for sale.

There was a floor for sorting stones up to one carat, from one carat to two carats and so on. These floors consisted of long tables at which sat qualified diamond graders, whose job it was to sort the larger stones according to colour and clarity. With a jeweller's loupe (the small eyeglass used to examine detail in jewellery) in hand, they would examine each stone individually, both internally for inclusions and flaws, as well as for the purity and intensity of its whiteness. The whiter the colour and the fewer the internal flaws, the more valuable the stone would be. It was an extraordinary sight to behold, and a job that required genuine expertise.

We eventually ended up in a section for rare and special stones. Specials are the one-off big stones and those of exceptional colours such as blues, pinks, and yellows. Into my hand was placed an extraordinary yellow stone of around a hundred carats, with an estimated value, I was told, of over a million pounds. The sickening exhilaration of the moment was a timely reminder of the seductive power of diamonds and corrosive impact they can have on the human soul.

I cast my mind back to being homeless in London, the rural poverty of Tanzania, Meron and Sarai and their childhood of prostitution and violence, and the women of Sierra Leone who turned gold into daily bread to feed their hungry children. I wondered how I had managed to travel so far from my origins as a campaigner. Here I was in the temple of the diamond. Everything was ordered and structured to pay homage to the smallest of stones whose carefully constructed liturgy had beguiled the world into believing this offering of the white stone to the woman by the man was a symbol of the purest love and intention.

The yellow diamond in my hand became a symbol, a timely reminder, that the power to seduce would never be far from the front door of my soul. I needed to tread carefully from now on. I was no longer in the little league of jewellery, playing around on the fringes of change, but had touched the murky soul of the jewellery trade. I was not sure I liked what I saw.

CHAPTER SEVEN

The Soul of Gold is Traceability

My story to date had been one of raw exposure to the forces that shape and define the whole of the jewellery trade, from the smallest and poorest miner in Sierra Leone to the richest diamond banqueting table.

I had journeyed through a landscape of immense contrast and had encountered some of the bravest and most creative people I could have ever imagined. CRED Jewellery, from its lowly beginnings of selling silver jewellery in an upper room, had pioneered an ethical gold wedding ring that was world-class as well as a world first. We had inspired others to follow in our footsteps, and I was flattered by the overtures of the powerful elites that governed the financial realities of the entire industry. But what had become apparent to me was the enormity of the challenge that we faced if we were going to prove that jewellery could be created without any form of exploitation.

So with this as a backdrop, we set ourselves the target of becoming the first jeweller in the world to be fully transparent and traceable across all our jewellery collections. We therefore needed a movement of jewellers who could move on from desiring to be ethical to creating the demand for ethically sourced products. We also would need an international platform capable of delivering fully transparent and traceable materials to the jeweller and ultimately the jewellery consumer. Clearly CRED would not be able to fulfil the entirety of my goal for an ethical jewellery market.

The popularity and interest green gold wedding rings were generating in the media meant I was now much busier with presenting the public face of ethical jewellery. Also I became a de facto spokesperson for ARM and the responsible small-scale mining movement that was now emerging. This left less time to focus on the pragmatics of running the business, which was a constant source of frustration to me. We were still a very small company and, like all small businesses, faced the constant pressure of cash flow issues, trading in and out of our overdraft. We had a balance sheet that did not add up when we took away the personal loans Ruth and I had invested into the company through remortgaging the house. On top if this was the general bureaucracy and paperwork all small business owners need to deal with.

It was becoming apparent that I needed a business partner or investor to help me over the hurdle of expansion. But given I had already been burned once by a business consultant, I was determined to be more diligent this time. I began to look around for a small angel investor who could bring critical business acumen to the company, so in my spare time (which I really did not have), I began to outline a new business plan in preparation for the future investor, whoever they might be.

In the UK there was now more than just CRED Jewellery producing ethical jewellery. Vivien Johnston launched her Fifi Bijoux luxury ethical boutique in 2006 and that was quickly followed by Ingle & Rhode's ethical jewellery, April Doubleday, and Oria Jewellery. A plethora of smaller designer–makers began to emerge, all of whom wanted to be as ethical as possible. What jewellers desperately needed was a secure supply of material that was traceable, audited, and able to be connected with the public. The Fairtrade Labelling Organization (FLO) had just the system and, importantly, they had the consumer trust that their process worked. But could it work for gold?

The Fairtrade label was a well-known consumer reality by this time, beginning to break out on supermarket shelves, and it had a polling of over 60 per cent consumer recognition. This kind of broad support and acceptance with the general public in the UK was unprecedented and the envy of all the other certification labels. But gold was not bananas, tea, or coffee. It was not an agricultural product, and Fairtrade Labelling did not have a reputation for working in the luxury goods market. So the challenge was: could Fairtrade certification work when applied to a high value luxury commodity such as gold? I believed it could, but we would have to start from the ground and build up. It would not be quick.

The reason why I believed Fairtrade was the right way to go boiled down to the strength of the certification system versus the more amorphous claims that were beginning to be made in the name of ethical jewellery. The word "ethical" was beginning to be used by more and more jewellers and could mean anything from "I recycle my plastic bottles in the workshop" to "I source my stones from a great community project in Africa". But how could a customer really know that what a jeweller was telling them was true?

What the consumer needed was a strong, trusted, independent verification system and a transparent standard that covered the source of the claim. This is what in the certification world is called "an independent third party verification system", and these were the very principles that the Fairtrade movement had been built on. So when I, as a jeweller, say to my customer, "This is Fairtrade gold," the customer does not just have to take my word for it; they can actually check the truth of my claim. They can see the standard for Fairtrade gold; they can check the audits if they wish. The independence comes from the fact that the Fairtrade certifier is not in any way connected to my business, or the business of the mining group I buy from.

So arranging a meeting with Harriet Lamb, the CEO of the Fairtrade Foundation, was a significant moment in the beginnings of Fairtrade gold.

I'd first met Harriet at Katharine Hamnett's house in 2003. I had known Katharine since the late nineties when we had collaborated on a T-shirt campaign for CRED on issues of child labour and ethical fashion. Katharine's award-winning status as an iconic British fashion designer included creating stonewashed jeans, the "Choose Life" Wham! T-shirt, and her famous "58% Don't Want Pershing" T-shirt that she wore when she met Mrs Thatcher at 10 Downing Street as a protest on the UK's continued addiction to nuclear missiles. She was prepared to put her mouth were her money was, and very good at getting her voice heard.

Katharine lived in a four-storey mansion in north London within earshot of Arsenal's Highbury Stadium. We sat sipping champagne in her kitchen, surrounded by copies of the *International Herald Tribune*, *The Guardian*, *Vogue*, and *Wallpaper*, with enormous bunches of dried and cut flowers washed in the glow of the colossal fish tank that made up half of her kitchen wall. We discussed collaborating on a collection of diamond and gold jewellery made from green gold, while waiting for Harriet and George Alagiah, the BBC news anchorman and patron of the Fairtrade Foundation, to arrive.

Fairtrade were in the process of launching certified Fairtrade cotton, and Harriet had come to discuss Katharine supporting the launch. Katharine, a committed environmentalist and supporter of pesticide-free organic cotton, was hoping the Fairtrade standard on cotton would ban the use of pesticides in the fair trade supply chain. I was introduced to the bubbly, effervescent Harriet, who was eager to learn about my work in jewellery and especially about my relationship with the environmental miners of Oro Verdé. Harriet and I hit it off instantly. We exchanged numbers and I agreed to get back in touch with her when we were in a position to have a solid conversation on creating Fairtrade gold.

It was with this growing movement of smaller jewellers and historic commitment from Fairtrade to explore the idea of gold in the background that later in that year I flew off to Peru and Colombia to attend the next rapid round of board meetings for ARM. I walked into a mini crisis, as our first interim manager had not delivered on our expectations, and had tried to wrestle power away from Catalina as the chair. I was despatched to let her know that we would not be renewing her contract and that she could no longer represent ARM. In the place of the outgoing naughty board member, a gold trader and refiner from France and a Peruvian small-scale miner who had a successful track record in advocating on behalf of small-scale miners in Peru were drafted in to help strengthen the existing ARM team.

We decided to formalize ARM around a vision that enshrined a set of values that promoted ecological integrity, transparency, and traceability in the supply chain, and create a set of standards that could be audited. Given the success of these ideas as demonstrated by Oro Verdé and CRED, we knew that there was a model we could build on. Also with the growing number of jewellers primarily in the UK wanting to go ethical we needed an organization that would be business-orientated and truly accountable. ARM came together around what became known as the Quirama Vision, which recognised artisanal and small-scale mining as:

> *a formalised, organised and profitable activity that uses efficient technologies, and is socially and environmentally responsible, that increasingly develops within a framework of good governance, legality, participation and respect for diversity, it increases its contribution to the generation of decent work, local development, poverty reduction and social peace in our nations, driven by a growing consumer demand for sustainable minerals and ethical jewellery.*[1]

These meetings were long, drawn-out affairs. The challenges of translating from Spanish to English and back again were always very frustrating for everyone. I found the preoccupation with procedures, processes, and protocols very boring, but it was the South American way. I respected the fact that ARM was a South American organization rooted in its cultural way of approaching life. But I was also aware that despite the rather mundane surroundings of hotel meeting rooms, we were actually laying the foundations of something potentially very progressive. Importantly, at last the small-scale miners saw that there was a group of people who took them seriously and wanted to work with them to improve the lives of their families and communities. I was delighted because I could see the beginnings of a process that could deliver traceable fair trade gold to the growing network of ethical jewellers.

The challenge, however, would come in how we could turn this into a system that would carry the respect of the international market. It was here that the principles of Fairtrade became important. I argued successfully that the world's most high-profile certification label could provide us with the legitimacy and market exposure we were looking for if we could create a standard for artisanal gold production.

We took the decision to begin a process across South America with miners that would lead to an artisanal gold standard. We shamelessly downloaded the generic Fairtrade standards from the FLO website, agreeing that the framework of the standards could be adapted to fit artisanal gold mining. We did not want to reinvent the wheel if we could avoid it. The FLO standards framework offered our newly appointed manager, Cristina Echavarria, a ready-made, tried, and tested technical framework that she could build the gold standard process around.

Cristina proved to be an amazing woman; her dedication and passion for artisanal miners was second to none. She brought the energy, knowledge, and expertise to the genesis of our project that we desperately needed.

I was despatched to go back the UK, contact Harriet Lamb, and open up discussions about working in a partnership to deliver mine-to-market certified gold. Upon my return from the ARM board meeting where we had unanimously agreed to pursue the Fairtrade model for building our standards and supply chain to jewellers, I gave Harriet a call and arranged a meeting.

The Fairtrade Foundation (FTF) had grown up since the early days of my campaigning on Fairtrade issues by wearing ridiculous banana outfits and giving press briefings outside Tesco, who, at the time, refused to stock Fairtrade tea and coffee. The FTF had won those fights, and now all the leading supermarkets stocked Fairtrade products. Fairtrade had gone from the margins of the UK market to being a mainstream high-street phenomenon.

With this hard-won success had come exponential growth, and the foundation was no longer a small operation. It had taken on the management structures and the departmentalizing of operations needed to service the corporate supermarket culture. This meant the Fairtrade Foundation in London and the Fairtrade Labelling Organization (FLO) HQ in Bonn, Germany, would have the institutional capacity to manage a turbulent, controversial, and potentially divisive product such as gold. Harriet had done an amazing job in creating the world's biggest fair trade market in the UK, and it was the logical place to start the discussions about introducing gold as a new product into the Fairtrade portfolio.

In all of my travels over the previous five years, I had dreamt of a systemic response to the entrenched poverty and exploitation at the heart of the jewellery industry. I had hoped for a business framework dedicated to using the potential of the sector to redistribute more of the wealth found in the gold trade back to the forgotten poor. We clearly needed a trusted framework that was pro-poor and that any jeweller or jewellery business could access, a system that would have the credibility and strength to govern a product as corrupting as gold.

I now seemed to have found a like-minded group of people from all aspects of the jewellery supply chain who shared this same simple vision. ARM was establishing the expertise in small-scale mining issues and, most importantly, the buy-in from the miners and in the Fairtrade framework, we had a skeleton on which to build a true certified supply chain, and the Fairtrade label had the credibility and consumer connections needed to establish a successful Fairtrade product in the market. That was the theory – now all we needed to do was to deliver.

But first I had to give a talk.

Edward Johnson of the Gemological Institute of America (GIA)'s London academy invited me to speak at one of their alumni events, which would include their current crop of gem students, on my now standard topic of Ethics in the Jewellery Industry. Arriving at their HQ in the early evening of 28 February 2007, I set up a presentation that consisted of the narrative around the plight of small-scale miners and their direct link to the jewellery industry, and I also included a few choice anecdotes from a recent trip I had taken to Tanzania at the back end of a family holiday earlier that month.

I had taken a week and visited two very different types of mining. One was the Williamson diamond mine run by De Beers, in the Shinyanga Province south of Mwanza. Williamson was the oldest working diamond mine in Tanzania, established in 1940 and later acquired by De Beers in 1958. Like the majority of African diamond mining operations, had been struggling to cope with the alluvial opportunists who would regularly break into the fenced-off lease area of the mine and prospect or look to steal whatever they could.

This kind of security issue is typical of what happens around large-scale mines. To be able to mine at all, they must often displace local people. Then, if the levels of beneficiation such as schools, health clinics, and clean water promised to the community by the mining company do not materialize, resentments quickly build up and the excluded communities take matters into their own hands in order to feed their families.

In the case of the Williamson mine, De Beers had recently come up with a very progressive approach to potentially resolving this long-term issue. They had begun the Mwadui Community Diamond Project and were keen for me to look at what they had been doing.

Travelling onto the mine site was like travelling back to the time of British colonial rule. The site was huge, with immaculately manicured lawns, flowers in bloom, and the rich red soil of Africa drinking deeply from abundant supplies of water. We drove past a chapel, shops, and numerous houses that I could only assume were residences for De Beers's staff and guests. I felt like I had wandered onto the film set of Out of Africa and at any moment I would be given an ice-cold Pimms and asked to dance the Charleston. On first appearances it was more of an African estate than a diamond mine.

It was a huge contrast to the small towns and villages that bordered the mine. These had mud buildings, intermittent electricity, poor sanitation, and inadequate education and water supply. It was another stark reminder to me of the minority "haves" and the majority of the "have nots" that underpinned the jewellery industry.

De Beers had set aside a section of land covered by their mining lease that was not viable from an industrial mining perspective. The local community would be entitled to access the diamond gravels if they were licenced to do so by the Mwadui project. De Beers would invest $2 million as in-kind technical support plus some cash alongside their knowledge of markets and pricing, to ensure that the local Mwadui miners got more than their current average income of $25 per month. This would help them break free from the network of traders, lenders, and loan sharks who preyed on the vulnerability created by their poverty.

With over 20,000 people dependent on a living from alluvial diamonds in the Shinyanga area, this project was well on the way to starting when I visited. The optimism in the air was tangible.

It seemed that this project had learned some vital lessons from the Peace Diamond Alliance and was likely to succeed where the PDA had recently and tragically failed; the diamond sites the PDA had invested into had not turned up significant diamond yields of worth and the funders decided not to continue the project, a fact that had only recently happened, some twelve months after my visit in 2005. De Beers needed commending for their response to the existing problem.

There was no point in my raising the obvious questions: "Why, after nearly fifty years of De Beers enriching themselves on the diamonds from Shinyanga, have the local communities not been lifted out of poverty, deprivation, and exploitation?" or "Why is it that only now, after the blood diamond scandals, that De Beers are taking a more structured and proactive approach to the alluvial diamond diggers poverty?" The fact was, De Beers were doing something and it should be supported.

It was becoming clear to me on my journey in the diamond sector that without the big diamond companies getting their hands dirty in this way, it was going to be virtually impossible to secure a traceable diamond from the hands of the alluvial diamond miners. I committed CRED Jewellery to being a future customer of any gem-quality stones that came from the Mwadui project. An internal goal of CRED Jewellery was to secure a source of gem-quality diamonds from the hands of the alluvial diamond miner that would complement our gold sources. Mwadui Community Diamond Project ticked a number of those critical boxes.

But the Mwadui project never happened. Within eighteen months of my visit, De Beers had sold the Williamson mine to a hedge fund based out of the British tax haven of Jersey. The project closed and another promising initiative failed.

Like all acts of Corporate Social Responsibility (CSR) in the mining sector, and the good intentions promised through them, the inherent weakness is that they are ultimately subject to the bottom line economics of the mother company. Corporate Social

Responsibility is not the same as local sustainable wealth creation and this has always been the biggest failure of the CSR philosophy. This failure in De Beers's CSR promises to the local communities was typical of every mining company I would see time and again on my travels. Promises would be made, hopes and expectations of communities raised, and then those promises would be broken. This in turn would lead to a re-entrenchment of the fatalism that exists in the foundation of the poverty mentality of the local communities.

The other initiative I visited was a gold-buying operation run by FBME Bank Ltd in the gold-rich Geita region. Kathleen Charles, who was working for the bank as a community liaison officer, invited me to visit a new project they were launching to build buying stations in this artisanal-dominated gold area of the country.

The idea was to introduce a safe, secure location in which small-scale miners could sell their gold. The bank would buy the gold at a reasonable discount on the London gold fix and also offer a secure banking system for the miners. This in turn would reduce the amount of cash in circulation and hopefully reduce the criminality in the area.

The miners would bring in their gold to one of the buying stations, and enter one half of the complex. Here they would be able to see the live gold price on a TV screen linked up to the Internet. On a blackboard, the discount daily buying price would be noted in Swahili, so pricing was fully transparent. The miner would hand their gold to the buyer across a security counter and metal grille where it would then be weighed and tested for purity. All of this was relayed to the front of the buying station via video camera, so that the miner could watch every step of the weighing to ensure that they were not being ripped off.

This was one of the biggest issues small-scale miners faced when it came to processing their product. The people that did the processing took small amounts of gold for themselves under the counter, or played games with the purity of the gold, thereby reducing the amount of money that miners were paid.

In the Geita project, once the weight and purity was decided, the miner would be given a receipt for the value of the gold, which could be credited to their bank account, paid to them in cash, or act as a credit note for the other half of the buying station that sold tools and equipment.

The model was simple and effective. Once the gold was bought from the miner, it was refined on-site to a pure gold bar and helicoptered out of the station to FBME's secure vaults in Dar es Salaam. FBME's plan was to open five of these stations around the region and to try to capture some of the thousands of kilos of gold that were coming out of the ground per month.

As we bounced and bumped our way through the rough terrain, we would stop every now and again to meet one of the miners working with FBME. It was the only time on my many travels searching for sources that I have ever had a gun pointed at me. I was trying to take photos of the journey as a record of my trip. A young man of what appeared to be late teenage years decided he was uncomfortable with this and pointed his rifle at me. I got the message and hid my camera.

The metaphorical drug of choice in the area for processing the gold was mercury, which has devastating effects on the environment as well as the health of the user. FBME was working with some of these miners to train them to use mercury properly, and through the equipment store was selling reasonably priced pieces of equipment called retorts. These would allow the miners to safely burn the mercury-enriched gold so they would not breathe in the toxic fumes released during the process. FBME were also helping to build proper secure concrete washing pools, so as the miners mixed the mercury and gold-enriched rock dust together in a process called amalgamation, none of it escaped into the water system that could then be drunk by the local population.

The real revelation on this part of my Tanzania trip was a chance meeting with a junior minister of the environment in the Tanzanian government who was also visiting the FBME system. The talk of the bush telegraph at the time was the collapse of one of the walls of the cyanide leaching pools at AngloGold Ashanti (AGA) Gieta Gold Mine that AGA referred to as a partial slope failure. This failure had caused a serious cyanide spillage and the temporary closure of the mine site while they attempted to clean up the mess.[2] The junior minister was very unhappy that this had happened and also very frustrated that he was unable to do anything about it.

I was confused and challenged him to use his authority as a minister in the government to go onto the mine site and inspect the damage. I was aware that the drug of choice for large-scale miners for the processing of their gold was cyanide, and was shocked when I heard from this minister that the Gieta mine used thousands of litres of cyanide a year to heap leach their gold production. Heap leaching is the industrial process in which gold-rich rock is broken into smaller rocks, heaped up into what should be a safe open-air construction, reminiscent of a huge rubber-lined shallow lake, and then sprayed with a mixture of water and cyanide. The cyanide leaches its way through the fine gold-rich rock, dissolving the gold from that rock. It is then trapped on the rubber lining and channelled to processing tanks. These processing tanks are full of charcoal that absorbs the gold-enriched liquid, which in turn is then burnt, leaving almost pure gold.

A wall collapse, such as the one on the Gieta mine site, is a major environmental disaster, as cyanide mixed with other chemicals can lead to acid mine drainage and highly toxic levels of pollution in the land, and also the local water systems.

The minister was quite right to be concerned, but the rest of the conversation was very revealing. He was not prepared to investigate the contamination as, he said, "I would lose my job." I pushed him on this statement, but that was all he was prepared to say. He was clearly scared of the implications of crossing AngloGold and the connections they had in the government.

As I told these stories to a packed audience at the GIA's London academy, I was aware that I was stepping into a world of unwritten dogma about the relationship between large-scale and small-scale mining. The unchallenged mantra for decades had been large-scale mining is good for jobs, good for an emerging economy, good for social development through Corporate Social Responsibility projects, and the way toward economic prosperity for a poor country. Small-scale mining is bad for the environment, promotes criminality and lawlessness, and undermines the national economy through its informal nature. In its crudest terms: large-scale is good and small-scale is bad.

As I came to the end of my presentation and opened the session to questions from the floor, a World Gold Council employee jumped to his feet, turned to face me directly, and exploded in a diatribe that started with: "There is no toxic waste in large-scale gold mining and all small-scale gold miners should be shot." He was incensed at the tone and content of my presentation, and flatly denied that what CRED was doing with our physically traceable supply of gold from Oro Verdé was possible. "The industry simply does not work that way," he continued. "What you are doing is impossible and cannot be trusted."

Geoff Field, from the British Jewellers' Association (BJA), who at the time was sceptical of the idea of fair trade gold in the jewellery world, had to intervene, and calmed the World Gold Council employee down. He explained that actually there were a number of very high-profile cases of large-scale miners polluting the environment. In Romania on 30 January 2000, the Baia Mare Aurul gold mine had spilled 100,000 cubic metres of toxic cyanide into the local river system[3] and in Peru the same year, the American mining giant Newmont's Yanacocha mine had spilled 150 kilos of pure mercury from its lorries in a number of villages near the mine.[4] Geoff also helpfully pointed out that the World

Gold Council might not want to be seen to be promoting in public the genocide of all small-scale miners in the gold sector.

I did not need to say anything after that, as the room waded into the poor man and rallied to my defence. It was the clearest indication yet of the scale of prejudice held in certain quarters of the industry to the idea of full transparency and traceability in the gold supply chain, and also the growing level of grass roots support that there was for change.

This unwritten prejudice concerning the small-scale miners would manifest itself again in a more subtle way through the Madison Dialogue. The Madison Dialogue was designed to promote communication and information sharing among companies, civil society groups, and others wanting to encourage better business practices, sustainable economic development, and honest and responsible sources for gold and diamonds. This dialogue was called for because of the growing pressure on the jewellery trade for better human rights and environmental practice. Earthworks, an American environmental organization, had arranged for the symposium to take place at the World Bank in Washington DC. I was invited to go by Steve Desposito, the director of Earthworks, to speak about CRED Jewellery.

The first I heard of ARM being invited was when Cristina Echavarria rang me to say that she and Catalina had been asked to attend, but there was no space on the agenda for the small-scale miners to speak personally to the delegates about the challenges they faced. It seemed that the great and the good of the jewellery and mining world would be assembled and once again would ignore the small-scale miners. We argued strongly that it is fine having PhD-level academics and consultants who are experts in small-scale mining at the event, but to be truly representative, the miners should be there themselves. After all, De Beers were being a given a platform, Rio Tinto would have a platform, the jewellers large and small were being given a platform, yet the voices of the small-scale miners were being deliberately discriminated against.

For me, the Madison Dialogue was a wake-up call to the not-so-obvious deficiencies in certain campaign groups and corporate companies alike when it came to small-scale miners. I was angry that the pioneering miners of Colombia and Peru would be denied a platform by a set of educated elites who thought they could represent their interests. The elephant in the room for our industry was the exploitation of the small miners, and it seemed that to avoid the harsh realities of our systemic failures, it was better to have experts rather than actual miners at the event.

More concerning was the fact that environmental campaigners did not want the actual miners there either. Responsible small-scale mining did not fit the negative stereotype perpetuated by green campaign groups and corporate mining companies. It seemed that this was the one area where large miners and green campaigners agreed.

These meetings were always far too sombre and formal and seemed to pride themselves on institutionalizing boredom, so to mitigate against a catatonic meltdown, I printed out half a dozen T-shirts with the slogan "Where are the small-scale miners?" on the front with the ARM logo to spice up the proceedings, packed them in my case, and, upon arrival in Washington, gave them to the ARM delegation to wear.

Having ARM and the recently established Diamond Development Initiative there was no more than a token nod at the problem. CRED and ARM were pointing out that artisanal and small-scale mining (ASM) was not a problem to be managed, but a fair trade business opportunity to be embraced, and this was the core message I put across in my presentation. Despite the huge amounts of money and power in the room, the only companies that were delivering on economic justice and environmental mining practices in jewellery were CRED and the handful of jewellers in the UK who were working with the small-scale miners who had formed ARM. The more established jewellery brands all treated small-scale miners as a charity problem, not as a business opportunity.

The Madison Dialogue represented the emerging politics of an industry that fed itself off its own sense of self-importance and preservation. I realized elements of the corporate green campaigning sector and the corporate mining sector needed each other more than they were prepared to admit.

Here we all were in the belly of the World Bank, an organization that actively supported large-scale mining, at an event paid for by the big miners and luxury jewellery brands whose aim was to create a talking shop that would maintain the dominance of the large over the small. We clearly needed a new way of campaigning for progress on environmental issues and human rights that emanated from within the jewellery sector. And in Marc Choyt I found someone who agreed with me.

Marc is an American jeweller based out of Santa Fe, New Mexico, who was making noises in the US market on ethical jewellery issues. Marc is a passionate, ebullient, erudite, elk-hunting advocate for the regenerative power of the jewellery industry. His dislike of the corporate dominance of the jewellery sector in America is matched only by his infectious passion for the artisan craftsman, silversmith, miner, manufacturer, and designer.

Through our email correspondence we had warmed to each other. Americans and Brits don't always talk the same language, but in Marc I felt I had a soulmate in the industry, whose only agenda was to seek the truth in the jewellery sector and work to see transparent and traceable supply chains created. I was deeply impressed by his integrity and his spiritual commitment to truth and justice. We found huge amounts of common ground, and it was refreshing for me to be able to talk with someone who saw jewellery through a spiritual lens first, rather than the more predictable secular economic one.

Marc took on coordinating the Madison Dialogue manufacturing working group, and would be the only participant at the meeting to deliver something tangible in an artisan manufacturing standard. We would become good friends as well as colleagues on the journey that would eventually lead to the establishing of Fair Jewellery Action (FJA) in 2007. FJA became for us an opportunity to combine our energy with that of the other myriad of jewellers from both sides of the Atlantic who believed that human rights and environmental justice provided a core foundation that should be at the heart of the jewellery trade.

CHAPTER EIGHT

We stand on the shoulders of voiceless giants who anoint our rubies, sapphires, gold, silver, and diamonds with sweat born from their exploitation, and we casually pretend they do not exist.

Throughout 2006 and 2007 CRED's profile as the leading ethical and fair trade jeweller placed significant strains on my workload and that of the team. We were getting more customers and that was good, but this in turn meant we had to buy increasing amounts of gold. With gold prices rising, plus a 15 per cent premium on Oro Verdé gold, there was considerable strain on the company's cash flow. Also the ceiling on Oro Verdé's production of about 10 kilos per year presented us with a future limitation on how much we could grow our business.

We were also being asked to make more engagement rings, adding to the strain on the company finances as well as continually challenging us to source diamonds from traceable sources. This was a very complex problem and needed continual attention. We finally settled on two sources. For our larger stones we started using Canadian diamonds, as they claimed to be traceable from mine to retail. Each stone came with a tiny laser mark that meant it could be traced back to the mine of origin. For the smaller stones we began working with Mike Angenent, a Dutch guy with a background in diamonds, who was building a supply chain of traceable stones from different mines under his Jeweltree Foundation certification system.

Buying larger stones from Canada was a compromise for us, as we desperately wanted to source stones from the small-scale miners in Africa, but could not find a rough diamond source that could be cut into good quality diamonds and would also be consistent. Therefore we had to settle for second best.

So I asked the head of one of the biggest diamond companies for a copy of the standards they were using in their cutting and polishing factory. I was told that they would not share that information, as it was intellectual property belonging to the company. I was assured, however, that the audits were done by Ernst & Young and that all their cutting factories were located in Armenia, Belgium, and China and were compliant with the company's internal standard. Also, to ring-fence their claims, they told me they would be fully compliant with the Responsible Jewellery Council standard on cutting and polishing. But the RJC did not have a standard that covered cutting and polishing. In short, their Canadian stones were traversing the globe, being cut in factories that had no transparent public accreditation, and would be compliant with an RJC standard that as yet had not been drafted.

I found this sort of ethical gymnastics and corporate reporting very strange, and it only served to fuel my already suspicious mind about the state of the corporate diamond companies' commitment to transparency. But we were now caught between a rock and a hard place and to build our little business we had to accept a measure of compromise on our own standards in order to take a small step forward on getting traceable diamonds.

CRED now had a number of wholesale customers in Britain and Ireland who wanted to sell our Oro Verdé wedding ring collection, which also meant a change in the way we were manufacturing our jewellery. We began to explore the idea of having our own dedicated workshop, rather than outsourcing the creation of our jewellery to individual jewellers. CRED was also getting asked to supply smaller jewellers with simple gold products such as the gold casting grain, gold sheet, and wire that bench jewellers use as the semi-finished gold material that they employ to make a finished piece of jewellery.

What seemed to be emerging was a multifaceted business opportunity offering ready-made wedding collections, a bespoke custom design jewellery service, and a wholesale business that supplied our collections to other independent jewellers. CRED had raised the expectations in the industry of an ethical product and was now living with the consequences of that expectation. Any jewellers nationally who aspired to be clean, green, and fair trade came knocking on our door asking for our help.

Alongside this, the workload emerging out of ARM started to increase as the team began to get to grips with creating the Fairtrade gold standard and build up ARM's capacity. ARM's consultative process under Catalina in the early days was impeccable, but when every email was accompanied by a document to be read and commented on, it became a daily ritual of poring over constitutions, processes, procedures, and protocols.

Cristina was equally making very good progress on building the South American process for the creation of a Fairtrade gold standard and she formed a standards committee, of which I became a founding member. Very quickly we began to see the outline of what Fairtrade Fairmined gold could look like: a gold standard that covered the organizational transparency and democratic foundations of the miners' groups. It included labour standards that addressed the child labour issues prevalent in mining and environmental protocols on how to mine ecologically, as well as the safe use of mercury and cyanide in hard rock mining. It would also have a trading standards section that would govern the financial issues of minimum price and the payment of a fair trade premium, as well as the traceability requirements that jewellers needed to sell with integrity. It was a complex document and required attention to detail and no small amount of time to input into with integrity.

I recognized that clearly there were not enough hours in the day to meet everyone's expectations so I rationalized my time to what I considered to be the most strategic issues. First we needed an investor or business angel who could put in cash and bring key business knowledge to structuring the company to meet the new set of challenges. Secondly, I wanted to improve the ethical performance of CRED Jewellery. The diamond issue continued to frustrate me and I went looking for help from Estelle Levin, a customer and expert in supply chain management, to build on our earlier work with the Natural Resources Institute. I asked her to create an ethical quality assurance framework for the company that would ensure our jewellery got even better than it already was.

Finally, I always made myself available to the press. I knew I had to cultivate a good relationship with them, not just for the sake of greater company profile, but also for the emerging ethical jewellery movement. An important part of delivering the demonstrable revolution in ethics in the jewellery sector meant giving what little time I had left to ARM, so we could achieve our stated aim of creating the world's first certified fair trade gold supply chain.

Being so foundationally associated with an idea such as ethical jewellery has its downsides. At times I struggled to separate my identity from the activity. As I became more of a spokesperson, I found it played havoc with my emotional state, and I would find myself taking things personally when people did not agree with me. This led to a dangerous volatility within me, and I had to constantly assess my responses to any particular problem. Ruth was a constant source of strength and often unfairly took the brunt of my ire as I vented about the exploitation I was witnessing, my feelings of powerlessness to do more about it, and my lack of an emotionally mature response to processing the suffering being meted out by an industry that did not seem to put the human condition before the profit margin.

No one likes a preacher ramming things down people's throats. However, I did not have the money that the corporate jewellery and mining sectors have so that they can spray the public with their particular version of reality. The only weapon I had to counteract their propaganda was my voice. I often felt a little like John the Baptist, a voice crying in the wilderness, marginalized, caricatured, but with a passion for transparency and traceability that were akin to the Baptist's addiction to truth and light.

I was plagued by insecurities and doubts about my own abilities, my convictions, and my public commitment to the idea of fair trade as the vehicle for delivering change in a deeply compromised industry. I was also a bad politician, and my principled unwillingness to do the small politics required in any emerging organization would ultimately prove to be the downfall in my relationship with ARM. I would look around the corner of the jewellery trade and see a mountain range of impossible ethical heights and would hear the still, small voice saying, "Keep climbing." Beyond the mountains I could see a landscape where jewellery was redemptive, transparent, and traceable; delivering a beauty that transcended not just its design and monetary value, but also human rights, justice for the oppressed, and environmental justice that honoured the creator of all things.

The biggest test of my convictions would come at The World Jewellery Confederation's annual Congress in Cape Town in early 2007. The Responsible Jewellery Council was asked by the president, Gaetano Cavalieri, to run a morning session dedicated solely to ethics in the industry. Given the historical bust-up between the two organizations, it was an act of refreshingly gracious generosity on Gaetano's part. I was asked to attend and be one of the presenters on the ethics panel.

It was the biggest platform I had as yet been given. The big guns from our industry would be there: Nicky Oppenheimer, the soul and principal owner of De Beers; the South African minister for mines; executives from across all sections of the gold

Greg and Hari Thapa, CRED's first jewellery community trade partner, in Nepal, 2003.

Ameriko Mosquera's green gold mine, Chocó, Colombia, 2004.

Greg and Catalina Cock Duque panning for gold in Chocó, 2004.

Greg watches a woman pan for gold in Sierra Leone, 2005.

Children working with
mercury in Quimbelete
pits in Relave, Peru, 2007.

Rubies confiscated from
Greenland miners, 2007.

Niels Madsen (front left) and Greg meet with the Bureau of Mines and Petroleum (BMP) in Nuuk, Greenland, 2009.

Left to right: Manuel Reinuso, Juana Peña Endara (leader of the Bolivian small-scale gold mining cooperative, Cotapata) holding the first ever 1 kilo bar of certified Fairtrade gold, Greg, Cristina Echavarria (ARM) holding the ten grams of Oro Verdé gold, and Harriet Lamb (CEO of the Fairtrade Foundation) at the UK Fairtrade Gold launch, London, February 2011.

Niels Madsen (centre) and friends on "Ruby Mountain" , Greenland, 2009.

Left to right: Colin Firth, Greg, Livia Firth, Lucy Siegle, and Ameriko Mosquera at the Observer Ethical Awards held in the Natural History Museum, London, 2011.

Greg shakes the hand of a man whose arm had been cut off by rebels during the civil war, Sierra Leone, 2011.

Mr Dave's derelict mechanized processing unit in the middle of the Nizi River, eastern DRC, 2013.

A small-scale gold mine on the Nizi River, eastern DRC, 2013.

and diamond industries from India, China, Thailand, Europe, and North America, as well as the big mining companies; and the different worldwide trade associations and members of the global industry press. I was aware it was a big event, but until I turned up I was not aware of exactly how big it was.

I knew it was going to be interesting as soon as I arrived at the hotel to be asked by the security personnel what I was doing at this private function. I replied I was here for the Congress and was one of the speakers. I was looked up and down in such a way as to question the truthfulness of my comment and sent over to the Congress reception. Once I had booked in, I was told I needed to be seen by the press secretary.

He was obviously uncomfortable with me. He said that as I was a speaker, I had to submit my corporate press photo for the website. I told him I did not have a corporate press photo, but he could use any of the photos from my online biography. He was not happy with this: none of the online photos available had me wearing a tie. I tried to explain to him that I did not own a tie. The poor man was clearly struggling to understand how this scruffy young guy had been designated as a speaker and, more importantly, what he was going to do, as I did not own a suit and a tie. He decided the best thing was to lend me a tie and take his own press photo, but when I pointed out that I would be wearing a Fairtrade gold campaign T-shirt at the event and that a photo of me wearing a tie and T-shirt would look even more ridiculous, his gaskets finally blew. He told me I could not take part in the event.

Once it was established that I had been flown all the way from the UK to take part in the Congress as a leading ethical jeweller, he finally relented and I was allowed into the main conference.

Over the next three days we would hear from ministers, Oppenheimer, Cavalieri, and others on every aspect of the jewellery industry from naming conventions on pearls and the threat of laboratory diamonds to the South African policy of beneficiation for artisanal jewellers. Our ethics section was scheduled for day two. So for the first day I wandered around feeling like a fish out of water.

The day of my presentation came and I was asked for my PowerPoint presentation. I explained I did not have one as I was not very conversant with this style of presenting, but I would just speak from behind the podium. I was the only small jeweller at the event, never mind the only ethical jeweller present.

As I stepped up into the pulpit of jewellery, I looked out on a sea of hundreds of impassive faces, the veterans of corporate conventions, dressed in suits and ties, all uninterested in what this little jeweller from Britain was going to say. It was a very surreal experience; I could see the faces of the power brokers looking at me, self-assured and confident.

For the few seconds before I began my talk, I had a flashback to India, the nameless women who mined the garnets, the miners of Sierra Leone who pounded their bodies in the merciless heat for a dollar a day. I could see the sons and daughters of African slaves, fighting for their very cultural identity against a remorseless enemy using gold to launder drug money in Colombia. These were the faces of the majority in our industry. These were the hands and feet who stood in the mud and sweated blood to dig out the treasures of the earth.

These were the families and communities whose stories had been twisted by mining companies to create a narrative that suited their economic model, so they could appear to be the only solution to the mineral resources of developing nations. These were the indigenous people who were always losing the fight against the corporate greed of mining companies who needed their lands to enrich their shareholders. These were the men and women whose stories of suffering and exploitation had been ignored by an industry who directly profited from their exploitation.

As I paused, I felt the anger well up inside of me. I let the last eight years of compressed frustration, raw emotion, real stories, names, places, injustices, poverty, hunger, slavery, and the misuse the beginnings of the ARM standards work in gold, our usage of the Fairtrade standard template, and, importantly, ARM's decision to go for a fair trade traceable supply chain. The challenge Harriet would face was persuading the Fairtrade network to adopt gold as a new product. This would not be easy, given the international nature of the FLO's governance and voting structure.

FLO is made up of the producer networks in Asia, Africa, Latin America, and Western consuming nations who use the Fairtrade certification label. She explained its rather slow wheels of administration would mean we would have to be patient as well as forgiving. But Harriet was an excellent champion for new products, and gold would be one of her biggest challenge to date. There was no guarantee, however, that the organization would say yes to such a controversial product as gold.

Nor was this newly found profile or fair trade activity in any way helping our small company. While Harriet was busy working with the Fairtrade movement, CRED Jewellery had hit a ceiling limit on sales; costs were rising, cash flow was tight, and the competition we had spawned was now having an impact on us. On one level I was not worried by the ethical competition, as I was confident that our new ethical quality assurance framework was going to help keep us ahead of the emerging competition. However, and more importantly, our sales had levelled off and without the business angel, I feared we would stagnate and get eclipsed by those who would steal the idea and, with greater investment, snuff us out.

I had already approached the Dutch ethical investment bank, Triodos, who liked our plan, but saw it as high risk because we were in the mining sector. They made us an offer to invest but wanted 65 per cent equity, an effective takeover, and so I turned them down. I spoke with Shared Interest, based out of Newcastle, who again liked our fair trade approach to jewellery, but struggled with the mining aspect. They were used to financing agricultural projects, and if they funded us on gold, they saw this as high risk and wanted to charge us interest rates that I was not prepared to pay. Again I said no.

The ethical investment houses' biggest problem was we did not have the FLO mark associated with our products yet. They all wanted the official certification mark on the jewellery. Although Triodos and others were ethical in their investments, they were risk adverse, and clearly we were a risky business.

My prayers were answered in the shape of a softly spoken stoic Irishman called Andrew Hunter. Meeting Andrew was like meeting a dormant volcano with a Dublin accent. He was a tall, quiet, reflective individual, yet underneath there was a fire that could be set alight by the brazen stupidity of injustice, which the jewellery industry could supply in abundance. I was introduced to him via an old friend, and once we had finished off the new business plan, I emailed it across to him and then arranged to fly to Dublin for a meeting.

Andrew had worked for the consultancy firm Accenture and had recently retired. He was a practising Christian who wanted to work with small struggling ethical businesses and help in turning them around. His background as a consultant ticked a big box for me: we needed a figure in the company that could work with the team to improve our internal business operation and mentor the staff. This was an area I confessed I did not feel qualified to input into, as I am no process manager and had recently been described by eco blogger The Gin Lady as "unmanageable".

The second investor was a city-based businessman who ran his own investment management company, and his enthusiasm for our company was encouraging. I explained I needed more than just money; I needed help to run the business and to grow it. I needed his time as well as money. Between them, it looked like I had plugged the gap, and we set about executing the new business plan. We opened a small workshop, hired a goldsmith, took on a designer and operations manager, and invested into branding, communications, and a new transactional website. It seemed we had negotiated the squeeze, got the investment needed to turn the corner, and, strategically, had introduced a higher calibre of businessman to the company.

Within a year of the investment, our carefully conceived business plan was in tatters. The sales increases that we had projected did not materialize. The problems stemmed from a number of sources and converged on us all at once. The problems with rising gold prices and increased competition from other ethical jewellers were intensifying. Some of those jewellers acted with little integrity and blatantly copied us. Also, the emerging national market for ethical jewellery, which was relatively small and located in the intentional green eco consumers, hit saturation point.

We also quickly discovered that many of the independent jewellers who had said they would take our wholesale collections did not really understand how to sell them to their customers, and the extra costs could not be properly justified. The wholesale market that had been indicated during our business planning just did not emerge. But what angered me the most and became a sanguine lesson in the behaviours of the business world was that having made the investment in CRED, part of the deal was I now needed all kinds of insurance packages, pensions products, and other sell-ins that were a part of the deal in getting the investment. I was worth more dead to the business now than I was alive.

Within a year of investing, the second investor was not happy, which was understandable on one level but unreasonable on another.

"What's happened to my money?" he cried.

I explained we had invested it according to the three-year business plan and, despite our diligence regarding the wholesale market, it was not emerging to the level anticipated. He wanted to pull out. He rang me and asked for my personal assurance that CRED Jewellery had a future: did I still believe it would come good?

My reply was simple: I had not come all this way with my dream of fair trade ethical jewellery to give up now. I empathized with his frustration that the business had not performed as we had all expected, but we needed to stay focused, make changes, and keep walking. He simply could not work out whether he had made a mistake or not by investing in us. Eventually he walked away, with Andrew Hunter offering to buy his shares. The deal was done and I now had a solid business partner who had proven himself steadfast in the face of adversity. Once again I found myself in the position where I had to sit with staff, make redundancies, close down the workshop, and strip the business back to its core essentials.

I was devastated. It was a very dark time for me. Publicly I maintained that all was well; we had the confidence of the industry and people continued to look to us for business leadership. But privately I wondered whether we were dead. Ruth and I had no more money to invest. Everything we had had gone into the vision we both believed in, but now the tightrope had just got a lot thinner and the merest puff of contrary wind would blow us off the line and send us tumbling into liquidation.

The pressure was enormous and I felt as if I was carrying the weight of expectations of Colombian miners, the market, the fair trade activists, and our staff, not to mention the entire vision of an ethical jewellery product.

The fear of failure can be paralyzing for anyone, and I was not sure I had the strength to keep going. A huge part of me wanted to give up and, in doing so, console myself that I had made more progress in proving that jewellery could be fair trade than anyone else in the world. But I also had to admit that there was a huge amount of pride in me. Emotionally I was raw, numb, turbulent, confused, frustrated, angry, and depressed.

But perhaps most concerning was the unbearable pressure I felt had finally transferred into the home environment. Living with me was like living with a miserable bear. I was bullish and short-tempered, and made Ruth's life a misery. I had become deaf to everything around me apart from my obsession with the apparent contradictions of our success and failure. I was in the deep well of self-pity. I had forgotten that life and love are more important than fair trade gold. Not for the last time would I stand at the bottom of my garden, look up to the stars, and pray, "Is this all there is?" with tears streaming down my face. I was probably having a breakdown but was too stupid to realize.

CHAPTER NINE

**We don't want your sort of people having
that kind of wealth.**

Quote from an official in the Bureau for Mines and
Petroleum, Greenland

It began with a phone call from a Californian-based geologist
and gemmologist called William, asking for the help of the now-
established Fair Jewellery Action to support the Inuit people of
Greenland in the fight to retain their traditional rights to mine
gemstones as they and their ancestors had always done.

William had been arrested in August 2007 and deported
from Greenland on the charge of ruby smuggling, which I
confess rather caught my attention as he was very upfront about
it. Everyone knows there is a lot of dodgy dealing and smuggling
in the gemstone industry, but I had never been contacted by
someone who actually told me that this is what he had been
accused of.

The accusation being made by the local ruby miners was
one of collusion between a Canadian mining company called
True North Gems (TNG) and the Danish-run Bureau of Mines
and Petroleum (BMP), who were responsible for administrating
the existing mineral code of Greenland. Apparently TNG and
BMP were actively discriminating against the local Inuit and
Greenlandic ruby miners. The indigenous people were arguing
they were unjustly being prevented from earning a living out of

138

the gemstones from their island. This criminalizing of the local miners was rooted in the colonial rulers of Greenland thinking they owned the mineral wealth of the island.

The authorities were saying the miners had never had the right to mine in the first place, so their grievances were unfounded and they were the victims of external agitation by greedy dealers. These were heavyweight accusations, and I was initially reluctant to get involved as I was unsure of William's motives for contacting me. Was he just a disgruntled ex-employee bitching to anyone who would listen, as True North Gems insisted? To be honest I had no idea.

During the beginning of 2008, as I shuttled between the UK and South America on ARM-related fair trade gold standards work, I corresponded extensively with William. As he sent me more and more information on the issue, the more I began to believe there might be a problem. He introduced me to Niels Madsen, Inga Bolette Edege, Tida Ravn, and others who lived in Greenland, some of whom had been arrested and had had their rough ruby confiscated. The Greenlanders invited me to visit Nuuk and some of the ruby mountains, attend community meetings, and meet with the officials who seemed to be at the centre of the conflating problem. I came to the conclusion that there was a real issue here and agreed to visit them in July 2008, in what would be the first of two trips within twelve months.

The ecological irony behind this story was that, due to global warming, the ice sheets of Greenland were receding and revealing pristine deposits of valuable minerals that could now be exploited by those who saw the opportunity. TNG had employed William to lead the exploration and operational expansion of this small Canadian mining company in Greenland.

William's work involved employing local indigenous people who were gemstone enthusiasts to help in this exploration. During this time he had trained them in simple geology, grading, sorting, and valuing the ruby stocks the company was discovering.

This complemented the traditional knowledge that the Inuit Greenlandic prospectors and carvers already had.

William successfully built a team of local people who discovered, through his tutelage, the international value of one of their traditional stones, the Inek Amak, or ruby. In doing so, they began to break out of the cultural stereotype of only finding a meaningful livelihood in their stones through native carving and selling to a non-existent tourist market.

William believed in creating a system that benefited the local people as well as the company and saw local empowerment as good company practice, as it would create a lasting legacy for Greenlanders that would outlive the involvements of the mining company. However, his employers did not appear share this view and, once William's team had mapped the extensive ruby deposits around the Aappaluttoq Ridge, they released the Greenland team from their employment. As William said goodbye to what had become a group of close friends, the team gave him a handful of their personal ruby to take home as a token of their appreciation for all he had invested into the people of Greenland. On 2 August 2007 William was arrested as he left Nuuk airport, accused of ruby smuggling, and his handful of rough ruby was confiscated.

Once word got out of what had happened, some of the recently aggrieved Greenland miners travelled down to the Aappaluttoq Ridge and, as an act of solidarity, began to mine and prospect for ruby around the TNG non-exclusive exploration site, convinced that William's arrest had been instigated by the management of TNG.

When TNG realized what was happening, they called the BMP, who in turn called the Danish police, who flew in helicopters to the site and arrested the ex-TNG miners on 16 August and confiscated their ruby. The authorities had, allegedly, broken the existing Danish mineral code, which entitled Greenlandic and Inuit people to hunt, mine, and fish, and the United Nations Declaration on the Rights of Indigenous People articles 4, 5, 8.2b, 19, 21, 26.1. The BMP then began to actively suppress the people's rights to earn a livelihood from collecting, cutting, polishing, and selling their ruby through a process of changing the law to prevent anyone on the island picking up a stone and selling it.

The miners were outraged at what they saw as collusion between TNG and BMP, to prevent them from earning a living from ruby mining. They felt they were on the receiving end of institutional racism, epitomized when one of the BMP senior officers was quoted as saying, "We don't want your sort of people having that kind of wealth." As a result, the 16th August Union was formed to fight for their personal rights, as native Greenlanders, to make a living from the gemstone industry. They wanted to stop the bureaucrats from Copenhagen attacking their traditional way of life, and to prevent them from cynically manipulating the mining law to discriminate against the creation of a vibrant gemstone industry in Greenland. This was the backdrop to my arrival in 2008.

Arriving in Nuuk's airport was like landing in a field station that had recently discovered tarmac. I climbed off the plane and was greeted by grey skies, cold Arctic air, snow-capped mountains, and a broadly inhospitable environment. With no passport control I wandered into the chaotic airport, through baggage control, crowded by native families eating fried chicken, drinking Coca-Cola, and talking in the oddly harmonious guttural and rhythmic tones of Kalaallisut, the Greenlandic native language. Niels Madsen spotted me from across the entrance hall, came over, and introduced himself, and we headed out into the greyness to the small waiting car. We drove into Nuuk to the Hans Egede Hotel, navigating around buildings that reminded me more of communist Russian proletariat tower blocks than the homes of people who were benefiting from the enlightenment of Danish architectural genius. It was a surreal introduction.

We instantly got down to business. Niels told the story of their arrests and release, of broken promises from TNG on cutting and polishing courses, and the lack of transparency in the Danish-run mining bureaucracy. His stoic demeanour meant it was not so easy to pick up from him the gravity of the situation. He seemed at times confused and a little apologetic for the trouble that he had caused as we wandered through the drab streets to Tida Ravn's house, where I would be introduced to the other members of the 16th August Union.

Tida was a journalist and was confident, almost strident, in her assertions of collusion between the BMP and TNG. She was a champion of Greenland and the rights of Greenlanders to the wealth of their own island, and was well versed in the politics of Denmark and Greenland. However, the story that finally convinced me there was a real issue here came from an old guy sitting in the corner. His name was Thue Noahsen.

Thue had worked for TNG and was one of the miners who had been let go by the management. He was a deeply quiet man and even his voice echoed the contentment that comes from being at peace with your environment. Thue had collected 4 kilos of rough ruby and had been given a permit by the Bureau of Mines and Petroleum to take this to Copenhagen to sell. As he passed through the airport, he was taken to one side and asked for his export permit. When he produced it, he was informed it was being rescinded by the Bureau on the grounds that he was collaborating with a known American ruby smuggler, and his ruby would be confiscated and deposited in the Greenlandic bank for valuation.

Every member of the Union had a story like this: export permits refused, product confiscated, and constant threats of legal action if members continued to prospect for ruby. A pattern of behaviour seemed to be emerging, and it was not a favourable one if you were an Inuit Greenlandic stone enthusiast.

The hidden secret of Greenland's majestic mountain scenery is its vast richness of gemstone that is available to anyone as you walk the landscape, and this is what Niels wanted to show me. He was keen to demonstrate that there is enough ruby for everyone, both large and small, to benefit and earn a living. So the following day we set off on a boat captained by one of the union members, Christian, to attend a community meeting in the tiny fishing village of Fiskenaesset and then visit a ruby field. Fiskenaesset was the HQ for the field operations of TNG and had become the focal point for the fallout between TNG and the host community. Niels and the Union had organized the meeting so I could hear from the community directly and talk about the ideas of fair trade in developing responsible small-scale mining for local communities.

Once our boat had turned away from Nuuk and began to engage the ocean ahead of us, the pure wild splendour of the Greenland landscape came into its own. The crystal-clear blue ocean, contoured by the jagged edges of the coastline, the crisp cold of the Arctic air, and a horizon full of pure white castles of floating ice imprinted themselves onto my imagination. The zigzagging between icebergs added to the sense of isolation. In fact, the pregnant silence, despite the constant thrumming of the engine and slapping of the waves on the boat, was the most potent aspect of the four-hour journey. While the locals sat in the warmth of the cabin drinking coffee, smoking, and listening to rock albums, I stood outside on the leeside in the cold wind, and drank in the vista with a reverence for creation and its creator I had never experienced before.

My newly found Inuit friends understood the innate relationship between land, humanity, and divinity, and this whispered conversation was enshrined in the very language they used to describe the harmonious connection in all life. TNG and the BMP seemed to be in conflict with this traditional Inuit world view, and to be unable to understand it, or the effects their behaviour was having. This was evident in their refusal to recognize that there could be an alternative way to develop the gemstone possibilities in Greenland. They seemed to believe in promoting neocolonial mineral rights to foreign companies, with no regard for local people and their sustainable livelihoods.

Arriving in Fiskenaesset was simply beautiful. Red, green, yellow, and blue timber-framed Scandinavian-styled buildings were dotted along the shoreline, home to the 200 or so residents. We were greeted by half a dozen smiling locals who grabbed bags – in fact, did anything they could to be helpful – and led us up to the house we would be staying in overnight. Outside my bedroom window was the ubiquitous football pitch with a couple of boys kicking a ball around in the freezing wind.

Our meeting was held in the town hall that night – or what should have been the night, as at that time of year in Greenland there was only an hour of actual nightfall, which really plays havoc with your body clock. Before the meeting, I had spent some time up on the mountainside praying and writing out what I wanted to say. On my way down, I collected a bucketful of sand from the village shoreline and deposited it next to my chair at the front of the meeting.

Our meeting was a long, measured, and thoughtful affair, very much reflective of the pace of life in the Arctic. In the middle of the gathering of fifty or more adult residents of Fiskenaesset sat three representatives from TNG. They were easy to spot as they were the only white faces (apart from my own) in a sea of intent and weathered locals.

Niels began by speaking of the injustice that had happened, the arrests, confiscations, and broken promises of TNG in not delivering on their CSR promises. He then spoke about the impending law changes being drafted by the BMP, a law that would take away the islanders' current rights to pick up a gemstone and make a living from it. He described how the BMP were going to introduce mining licences, charge fees, give exclusivity and priority to bigger mining companies, and, in doing so, erode the current rights the population had to earn a livelihood from mining according to their traditional ways.

Niels and the 16th August Union were not against large-scale mining companies. This was not an anti-corporate campaign;

rather, it was a campaign to redress the injustices of illegal arrests and also to secure the rights of every member of the 57,000 population of the island to make a living out of the gemstone industry if they so chose.

"We can peacefully exist with True North and other mining companies, but not if we are criminalized by the BMP and persecuted for owning a ruby and wanting to make a living from this business," he stated.

The disempowered miners and their communities were trying to find their voice in the face of a bureaucracy that oversaw a mining law written by officials who did not represent the interests of the Greenland people. It reflected a basic clash of world views. The Western mindset sees ownership and possession as a right. The indigenous world view is one in which land cannot be owned, but rather it nurtures us all and we have responsibility to work with it, not against it.

There was also clearly a problem with what I call the colonial stereotyping of the local people. The Danish authorities had never been bothered about local people working with ruby when they were carving it into images of whales, musk ox, and other items relating to Inuit life in the Arctic, and selling these artefacts to the tourists. In fact they even paid for the Greenland Stone Club (another Greenlandic club of gemstone enthusiasts) to attend the world's biggest gem fair in Tucson Arizona. But once the locals found out the true value of their ruby and wanted to cut and polish it themselves and sell it to the international market, the authorities began to act against them earning a living from it. The directors of TNG and the mining bureaucrats were blind to the impact they were having on the locals.

After my short talk on fair trade principles and expressions of solidarity with the people of Fiskenaesset and the 16th August Union, we then heard from every person in the meeting willing to speak. The meeting spoke with one voice. They wanted to live peacefully with True North, to retain their ancestral rights to ruby, and to learn how to earn a living from these stones. They were concerned about the need for employment for their children and young people, and shared an overall incredulity at how the Danish authorities and the Canadian mining company were behaving in having their people arrested.

Symbolism is a powerful communication tool and my parting contribution was to pick up my bucket of sand and pour it on the floor of the meeting in a long line from one side of the hall to the other. I told the meeting the line of sand represented their aspiration to work with ruby to earn a livelihood and that it was symbolic of all of their words of hope that had been expressed in the meeting.

"If you support the idea and principle of the indigenous right to mine gemstones in Greenland and to earn a livelihood from that activity, I ask every person in this meeting to rise to their feet, if able, and to cross the line of sand."

I stood back and waited while the translator finished explaining what I had just said. The room went silent for a moment and then, toward the back, an elderly woman rose to her feet and slowly walked to the line. She stopped for a second as though meditating on the action she was about to take and then reverently crossed the line. One by one, every resident present in the meeting rose and crossed the line. One old man hobbled up to it with two walking sticks and, with a look of sheer delight and joy upon his face, jumped as high as he could, landed on the other side, and raised his hands in the air as though he had won the 100 metres at the Olympics.

Sitting in the middle of the room, still in their seats with a slightly perplexed look on their faces, were the three representatives from TNG. It was clear to everyone in that small fishing village that, despite the rhetoric that they were a good community relations company, TNG were no longer on the right side of line.

Back in Nuuk, we spent a few days in meetings with the Inuit Circumpolar Council, the local press, labour union officials, and, most importantly, the BMP, who were at the epicentre of the gemstone crackdown. One was a caseworker in the BMP overseeing the True North prospecting and another was the BMP lawyer charged with rewriting the mineral code.

The caseworker spoke at length on how the current mineral act did not permit Greenlanders to use semi-precious stones, as these belonged to the royal family of Denmark. He refused to answer questions regarding the arrests, why people such as William had not been brought to trial, or why True North's ruby had been given a low value for export purposes by an unqualified gemmologist from Thailand who had no background experience in valuations. Nor did he explain why the same unqualified gemmologist had overvalued the gemstones confiscated from members of 16th August Union. He stood by the party line that all semi-precious stones were the constitutional property of the Danish Crown and they had no other option but to act against the miners as they had broken the law. The BMP lawyer spent the entire time fidgeting like a chipmunk on speed and was silent throughout.

I left my first trip to Greenland with a sense of conservative optimism. I felt we had made our case for the rights of indigenous mining in a good way. We certainly had the backing of the community that was being directly affected by the ruby issue. But the complex woven cords of colonialism, power, and apparent obfuscatory behaviour of the BMP meant we were a long way away from getting to the truth of what we were now calling "the apartheid ruby" on this trip. As we prayed together the morning of my departure, we asked the God of Justice to bless the land and its people. I promised them I would return the following year to continue Fair Jewellery Action's support of their cause.

There is no doubt my first trip was followed by a level of energy and activity that was unprecedented in Greenland on the issues of gemstones. Within weeks, the Union had organized a public demonstration against the BMP calling for ruby rights. A part of their protest was to start a petition supporting their claim to mine ruby and for these rights to be enshrined in the new law. Within a matter of weeks, the Union had over 4,000 signatures supporting them, which, given the population of the island is only 57,000, was very impressive. The Union also launched their own website (www.freegreenlandruby.com) and organized a public rally outside the parliament building, calling on the government to respect the rights of local Greenlanders to mine, own, and make a living from gemstones.

Back at home I began to get abusive emails from an investor in True North Gems in reaction to my blog posts on my trip. He accused Niels and his friends of being "claim jumpers, a band of radicals who are trying to steal TNG rubies and a group of melodramatic half-Inuit who know nothing of traditional culture". The ranting went on to accuse me of being an economic terrorist because I was a jeweller and wanted to steal the ruby for myself, that Marc Choyt and I were in fact partners in crime with William, and that William was both a thief and liar. The vitriolic emails only served to confirm to me that TNG might in fact have questions that needed answering in their dealings with the mineral authorities in Greenland.

The following June, 2009, many Danish politicians and royal dignitaries gathered to celebrate Greenland's "Nearly Independent from Denmark" celebrations. The BBC news that morning headlined with the following:

> The Arctic island of Greenland is assuming self-rule, in the latest step towards independence from Denmark. The move follows a referendum on greater autonomy in November. It will see Greenland take a greater share of revenues from its natural resources. The local government is taking control of the police and the courts. Greenlandic – or Kalaallisut – becomes the official language.[1]

There had been a recent election and the socialist Inuit Ataqatigiit party had swept aside the pro-Danish social democratic ruling party Siumut of Hans Enoksen. As I stepped out into the chill of Greenland's mid-summer, the optimism in the air transcended the Greenlandic natural stoicism. Wandering around Nuuk with Niels, Tida, and others from the Union, I was constantly meeting members of the new parliament.

The newly appointed finance minister, Akitsinnguaq Olsen, in particular, was friendly, engaging, and openly interested in talking about the future of the mineral resource. She had heard the story of the ruby protests and that locals had been arrested, and was deeply concerned. Importantly, the new prime minister, Kuupik Kleist, and his energy minister, Ove Karl Berthelsen, had ordered the BMP director to meet with the 16th August Union, in the hope it would lead to a breakthrough in what had become an impasse on the ruby issue. It looked like the wind might be blowing in the direction of the Union.

On 22 June, the small-scale miners and I met with the BMP. This was itself a breakthrough. Up until the recent change of government, members of the Union had been treated as criminals. Ever since their arrests, Union members had been trying to meet with the director of the BMP, a man called Jørn Skov Nielsen. Nielsen had always found a reason not to meet Union representatives. He had now been ordered by the new government to meet face to face with the very people his department was responsible for criminalizing.

As we arrived at our meeting, it was clear some things had changed and others had not since our encounter with BMP officials the previous year. On one side of the table sat Jørn Skov Nielsen and the lawyer whose fidgeting and fiddling throughout the meeting was as off-putting as it had been a year ago. Also a geologist, another lawyer, and two young men who were caseworkers, joined us. The scene was set: six white Danish men and the 16th August Union, who were a mixture of local small-scale miners, a female journalist, an Inuit activist, and me.

Jørn Skov Nielsen instantly seized the agenda by outlining the nature of the discussions. I could see he and some of his team were not enjoying the meeting they had been ordered to attend. He talked about the new law, how he wanted the Union to have input, how there was only a short deadline, and that they would give us all a copy of the new draft law within two weeks, but only in Danish and Kalaallisut. In short, he wanted this group to read, understand, officially comment on, and follow through in writing with any amendments within a four-week period. The government might have changed but the institutional bureaucracy hadn't. What appeared as a concession was in fact a further illustration of the gulf between the two sides. Union members were being forced into a totally unreasonable timeframe on comments. It was a political tactic I found difficult to swallow.

I asked a series of questions:

"What is your team's experience in small-scale community mining issues?"

"None," Nielsen replied.

"Who are you using to help you shape the small-scale community mining aspect of the law?"

"No one."

"What budget have you set aside to secure equal rights and representation for local miners in the new law?"

"None."

I was agog at how little Nielsen and his team knew about small-scale mining and gemstones. This was further compounded when a BMP official talked about the irresponsible use of cyanide by small-scale miners and why they could not be trusted to work environmentally. I pointed out that cyanide is only used in gold mining, and there were no small-scale gold miners in Greenland. The Greenland miners were gemstone miners who used no chemicals at all.

This group of men had no experience in the issues they had been charged to write laws about. I was equally shocked that they had not even bothered to find out about the local small-scale gemstone activity they had criminalized. All their information came from TNG, who had a clear vested interest in keeping locals out of the gemstone business. The only argument they could generate against the ruby miners was a general textbook and anecdotal narrative from their background in servicing large-scale mining companies, who normally despise small-scale miners and hold deep-seated prejudices against them, such as our friend from the World Gold Council had expressed at the GIA meeting.

Progress began when Nielsen admitted that they needed help. I had already pre-negotiated the services of an excellent lawyer, Laura Barreto, who had extensive knowledge in shaping responsible small-scale mining law in a number of African and Asian countries. She would add her professional voice to the process. Nielsen acknowledged that budget could be allocated to the law making process to ensure the best legal outcome for the small-scale ruby miners, which was later confirmed to Laura in an email from a BMP lawyer. Nielsen talked about proceeding in "a spirit of good faith" and we ended the meeting on a very positive note. I believed we had a breakthrough, and the Union members felt that for the first time they were getting traction with the mining bureaucracy.

We all agreed to speak to the BMP again upon my return to the UK, so we could to arrange the details of how Laura could assist the BMP in securing a law change that would benefit everyone in Greenland.

With what we believed to have been a very constructive meeting behind us, we headed out to what I called in my subsequent blog postings "Ruby Mountain". I cannot begin to describe the sense of sheer exhilaration I get when I climb a mountain. As we approached Ruby Mountain, its face stretched up to breathtaking snow-capped heights from the depths of the crystal-clear waters that are fuelled by the 50,000-year-old glaciers further up the fjord. The icebergs were busy sculpting island playgrounds of refracting azure blue for sea trout, seal, and whale to play in.

As we jumped off the boat onto the shoreline, the mountain climbed up and away from us, parted down the middle by a cascading waterfall. "Ruby, ruby!" was shouted across the beach, and Niels handed me a piece of stone peppered with ruby crystal. Even the beach offered us its riches – moonstone, garnet, and black tourmaline were just a few of the gems we found within the first ten minutes.

This was a typical field visit for the Union ruby lovers. It meant a boat trip to the area, with backpacks loaded with food, a small hammer and chisel, loupes for examining the crystal formation of discovered gems, and pliers to extract them. This landscape is heaven-sent for small-scale gemmologists. Its location is breathtaking, its terrain wild and rugged yet warmly inviting.

I understand why my Inuit friends are so reverent of creation. They simply get it because they are not divorced from it. The accusation from the team at the BMP that local Greenland small-scale miners would be bad for the environment was simply rooted in ignorance. Here were guys who actually cleaned the beach of stray fishing tackle, rope, and plastic as a matter of course.

A ruby from the hand of the Inuit is not only radiant in its natural state but infused with love, passion, and this deep reverence for creation. This is exactly what jewellery should be about: the beauty and the joy of a treasure found that is then mirrored in the face of the customer who wears the treasure.

All day we traversed the mountain and it acted more as our playground than a mine site. It was truly majestic.

At the end of our time on Ruby Mountain, we gathered around a small fire at the base of the mountain and tucked into the traditional Inuit delicacy of whale meat, flash-fried on heated stone, with mountain herbs and a little garlic. It was the finest steak I have ever eaten and as moist and succulent a meat you will ever taste. As the glaciers gently drifted past, the sea trout jumped and played in the small bay before us, and we breathed in the clear mountain air, I knew I was tasting a little piece of paradise.

The open-handed conversation about creation included those of us who could be still and silent enough to be embraced by the moment. It was in this moment we all shared our dreams for an inclusive reverent system in Greenland and for a ruby from the local people that would be mined in an environmentally sensitive manner; a ruby that would create jobs, forge a new national economic opportunity, and become a symbol of nationhood. The Ruby Mountain was happy to share all he has, but not so keen to be owned by anyone. After all, what intelligent person can claim to own a mountain? Ridiculous.

In Greenland (as I had witnessed in Colombia), I began to see the possibilities of the jewellery trade as a vehicle for real social and environmental restoration. If only we could get the lawmakers to understand the opportunity.

The emotions my trips to Greenland stirred in me did not disappear on my return to the UK, and I was initially optimistic. Laura Barreto was in London for a series of meetings we would be holding regarding the partnership contract between ARM and FLO, and I had arranged for her to stay with friends in the Docklands. Our intention was to follow up on the promises of the BMP. For two days Laura and I talked at length via Skype and email with Nielsen and the BMP lawyer about our agreement for them to fund Laura to shape the law to reflect the wishes of the Union for a more inclusive mineral code. Laura offered them a fantastic rate for her input.

However, it soon became apparent that budget constraints meant they did not in fact have the power to honour their word to the 16th August Union. This was made clear through our follow-up correspondence, as they told us the Greenland Audit Office would view the BMP spending money on securing the services of a qualified lawyer who had links to the Union as unethical.

The 16th August Union were devastated. The Union had trusted the words of Jørn Skov Nielsen, that the budget would be there and the money be found to pay for Laura's services. The BMP then sent an official letter to all the arrested miners asking them to accept a fine of 5000 DKR in return for the case being concluded. This would be an admission of guilt and would legitimise the BMP's actions. The miners refused and the case has still not gone to court (six years later). They also reinforced their original timeframe on the consultation of the new law, expecting the Union to reply in detail within less than four weeks, knowing full well they now did not have the legal expertise to do so. For the Union it was just heaping up more bureaucratic obstacles to prevent the Union members from achieving their desire of a vibrant gemstone industry in Greenland.

After nearly two years of work to secure the rights of Greenlanders to mine, own, transform, and sell the gemstones on the world market, the bureaucrats and lawyers are still suppressing the rights of the peoples of Greenland to earn a living from the natural resources of their land.[2]

The Danish authorities never followed through on William's arrest and the confiscated ruby still sits in a bank vault in Greenland, with no clear judicial process in place to return the confiscated property to its rightful owners. The arrests of the miners themselves on 16 August 2007 turned out to be illegal, as prospecting for ruby or any other coloured gemstone at the time was totally legal, given the TNG site was constituted under a non-exclusive exploration licence. Also, in November 2009 the Ombudsman of Greenland ruled that the BMP had acted outside their authority and the law in ordering the police to arrest the Union members.

CHAPTER TEN

**You have not come this far and fought this
hard to give up now!**

The creation of certified Fairtrade gold and the challenges we were
facing to make this happen cannot be underestimated. It would be
a monumental feat, undertaken by a small group of people who
had a vision for the transformation of the small-scale mining
sector from being vilified as irresponsible by large-scale miners
to being accepted as a credible and responsible way to earn a
living. Alongside them worked a growing group of jewellers, who
believed that the innate beauty of jewellery rested in its power to
transform the lives of the poor and grace the environment with
the dignity and reverence that it deserved.

This process also became a microcosm of the internal politics
that takes place in a new organization as it begins to become more
successful.

Back in January 2007, Catalina, Cristina, and I bounced
through the northern edge of the Atacama Desert in southern
Peru. We were hosting, on behalf of ARM, the first official visit of
FLO to a number of the ARM partner fair trade gold pilot mines,

Our first stop was at a mining cooperative called Aurelsa in
the small desert mining town of Relave. Chris Davis was the
head of producer relations at the Fairtrade Foundation, and had
been tasked by Harriet Lamb to lead on integrating gold into the
portfolio of Fairtrade products.

Just getting this far had been a fight within Fairtrade. Since our earlier discussions about forming a partnership between Fairtrade and ARM, Harriet Lamb had gone back to her board in the UK and the international body based in Bonn and proposed the idea. Not everyone was in favour, and she had to work hard to persuade the Fairtrade movement that it would work. Some argued strongly that extraction industries should have nothing to do with the Fairtrade movement; they were too risky and might detract from the core commitment of Fairtrade to agricultural producers.

As a veteran Fairtrade campaigner, Harriet knew how to present the reasons why the artisanal mining sector needed Fairtrade intervention. Small-scale miners are some of the poorest people on the planet, and given that Fairtrade's commitment is to lift communities out of poverty, small-scale mining is a natural sector for Fairtrade to be involved with. Whether poverty and exploitation is in bananas, coffee, tea, cotton, or gold, the benefits that Fairtrade principles could bring to the miner–producers and their communities meant FLO had a moral commitment to exploring the possibility of making gold a Fairtrade product.

The deal clincher in this argument happened when Catalina came over to meet the Fairtrade people in London to present the newly established ARM and the work that we had begun in creating a standard that could be applied to small-scale gold production. Some people at the meeting attacked Catalina very aggressively as she presented the simple idea that small-scale miners should be allowed to earn a legal living from their work. The detractors dogmatically accused ARM of trying to replace the trade unions' role in representing the rights of mine workers, and of promoting some of the world's worst mercury polluters as being worthy to receive development assistance. One of the UK's leading development agencies stated they would not support Fairtrade gold on the grounds that small-scale miners should not benefit from economic development assistance because of their appalling track record in polluting the environment through the use of mercury.

It was a hot and fractious meeting. The first I heard of it was when Harriet rang me to let me know how well Catalina had handled herself. Her grace under pressure had teased out the internal opposition in certain sections of the fair trade movement, and her refusal to get involved in a slanging match had won her many supporters on the Fairtrade board. Harriet was deeply apologetic on the phone and reaffirmed her personal commitment to making Fairtrade gold a reality.

With the support of the chair of the board, Fairtrade Foundation agreed to undertake a feasibility study on the proposition, and Chris Davis was duly despatched to visit the mines thinking of going Fairtrade.

Relave is a small town of some 2,000 people. It is exclusively dedicated to mining gold. There is no other reason for its existence. With one road in and one road out, it is around two hours' drive from the main Pan American highway that skirts the Pacific Ocean, and it nestles between two high gold-rich mountains. Everything about Relave shouts of a hard-earned living from the dust of the earth. Well, everything apart from the smiles of the people.

As we drove into the town, the security guards stopped us and registered us as visitors. They were also checking for alcohol. The town council had banned alcohol, as its consumption was having a very negative effect on the lives of the people. Anyone who has worked in the mining industry knows that miners can drink in quantity, if not quality, and the consequences of this drinking is often violence toward each other, family, and friends. Since alcohol was first banned, the violence in the town had almost stopped completely.

We introduced Chris to the Aurelsa mine. He met the eighty-eight members of the cooperative, who took him deep into the heart of the mountain, where their gold was being extracted. The miners told stories of how they used to be exploited by traders further up the valley, who prevented them from reaching the coastline for basic provisions unless they sold their gold cheaply to their designated middlemen. They had to fight to get themselves organized, as local vested interests did not want an organized group of miners in Relave – disorganized and informal artisanal miners are easier to exploit.

The fledgling Fairtrade and Fairmined standards process that ARM had started with Aurelsa and other Peruvian gold cooperatives had already begun to reap the rewards of better administration and better organization within the cooperatives, and had helped to increase democratic participation and gender equality. The health and safety aspect of all mining is always one of the top priorities for miners, and working with some of the mining engineers that ARM had introduced meant simple things such as rehearsing evacuation procedures, plain signage in the mine, monitoring the flow of air through the tunnels, and clear protocols for blasting new seams of gold. All added toward a professional mining operation that could be measured and then incorporated into what would become the Fairtrade standard.

A key to the development of Fairtrade standards for gold was the very real hot potato of chemical usage. In Peru, all the mines that ARM was now working with used cyanide to process or leach the gold from the crushed rock, and despite it being the best and most cost effective way to extract the gold from the hard rock ore, cyanide is an ugly chemical and not a good ingredient in the romantic story of the pure gold ring that is told to the general public. Also, cyanide leaching can be very dangerous and damaging to the environment if not done professionally and safely, as I had witnessed in Tanzania.

The Fairtrade gold standard would have to insist upon all certified producers following the International Cyanide Management Code[1] as a model of best practice. The miners stressed they wanted to work in the safest possible way. They had no desire to cut corners. Health and safety alongside the maintaining of a quality water supply were paramount to an underground desert mining operation.

Chris was also able to compare and contrast the progress that Aurelsa were making with some of the other local gold operations. Wherever you walked around this little town, you would see small pits of water with large granite boulders sitting in the middle of them. Attached to the top of these boulders was a long plank of wood, and on each end were usually two boys holding onto a bamboo handrail, rocking the granite block in a seesaw motion in the nearly overflowing pit of water.

These "Quimbelete pits" represented the other way that gold was processed from crushed rock. Into the water would be poured gold-rich rock dust and a large quantity of mercury. The continual rocking motion would amalgamate the gold with the mercury. After a few hours of this in the baking hot sun, the water was removed and the mercury scooped out by hand and taken to a kitchen where it was burned to separate the mercury from the gold.

Horror! No protective clothing, no gloves, no breathing equipment, child labour, mercury spills on the ground, and the uncontrolled and destructive burning of mercury in enclosed spaces without safety equipment. And to cap it all, toddlers and young children played next to the pits in the mercury spills. It was enough to convince Chris Davis that despite the well-rehearsed arguments for why Fairtrade should not be involved, this kind of malpractice still needed to be stopped.

As we drove home that evening, the setting sun turning the desert into a landscape of fire and shadow, Catalina, Chris, and I discussed the headings of a Memorandum of Understanding (MoU) that the two organizations would sign as a commitment to our working together to create a model of Fairtrade excellence. We would start a formal process of negotiation to enter into a partnership, and ARM and Fairtrade would begin to bring their standards committees closer together to work on completing the gold standard. It was a very exciting trip and represented another key step toward the dream of Fairtrade gold.

For much of the next eighteen months, the long and slow protracted negotiations to secure the partnership between ARM and FLO would dominate my life. Not everything was rosy in the garden of ARM. With ARM having signed the MoU with FLO, the process for aligning the two organizations began in earnest, but first we had to deal with the announcement that Catalina wanted to step down as chair of ARM.

Catalina told me she wanted a challenge beyond artisanal mining and had been headhunted to run a new peace-building civil society group in Colombia. As she explained the opportunity to me, it was obvious she had no real option. She could not turn down the chance of being a part of bringing peace to her war-torn country. This was a big loss for ARM, as she had overseen the formation and establishment of the organization and was able to command the confidence of the market, the miners, and the campaign groups, as well as the funding organizations that had been supporting ARM up to this point. She had also managed to hold the simmering tensions of the board in check.

For some time now, ARM board meetings had not been easy affairs. All boards have their problems, discussions, and disagreements, and usually this leads to a stronger internal debate that should deepen and mature the vision of the organization. But in the case of ARM, this was not turning out to be true. Signing the MoU set off a string of internal anxieties about ARM the institution. Would it lose its unique role in shaping the debate around small-scale mining? Would FLO steal all its ideas and then dump them? What would happen if the partnership did not work?

ARM's work of creating standards for small-scale miners meant it needed to become a bigger organization, and this process of institutionalization was throwing up issues within the organization that I was deeply uncomfortable with. It started with a series of subcommittees that all consisted of the same people. Also, now that we were in protracted negotiations with FLO about a three-year partnership, certain people on the board would not talk to other people in FLO if they considered them to be of lower rank. It was starting to become a bureaucracy, rather than the dynamic service organization that had been launched a few years earlier.

What was most concerning, however, was when the board took the decision to stop making itself accountable to what was called, in charity-speak, the Stakeholder Alliance. When ARM had launched, it was established by a number of different groups such as Oro Verdé and CRED Jewellery, who were some of the stakeholders in the alliance. This broad group appointed the board and gave ARM a democratic mandate to represent them all to the rest of the world. The ARM board would now take all its decisions internally and consolidate power into the hands of the board itself. It moved from being a democratic organization accountable to its alliance members to being an organization whose board would appoint its own members without a vote from the stakeholders.

If it all sounds confusing, it was. It now appeared to me the biggest potential threat to us succeeding in launching Fairtrade gold was no longer the detractors in the wider industry or environmental campaign groups, but a few people on the ARM board who saw Fairtrade gold as a threat to their business model. I was disturbed by the moves within ARM and the obvious shift to a more autocratic culture. ARM publicly promoted transparency, organizational democracy, and accountability, yet internally was moving in the opposite direction.

But the most acrimonious debate by far within ARM was its position regarding traceability in the Fairtrade gold supply chain. Most consumers don't think about how a product is created when they decide to buy it. This is especially true with jewellery. It is a luxury product, and people buy it for emotional reasons, or because they think it says something about the sort of people they want to be – or to be seen as. There is a logical assumption that what you are buying says what you want it to say – I love you.

ARM had been founded upon the success of organizations such as Oro Verdé and CRED Jewellery and the traceable nature of the supply chain. This very radical idea had been unheard of in the gold business until CRED and Oro Verdé had delivered it in 2004. We had all argued forcefully, with people such as the Responsible Jewellery Council, Fairtrade, and environmental campaign groups, that part of the corruption in the gold industry was the systemic lack of traceability, and we were going to be different.

However, the trader on the board of ARM argued against this. Gold is simply a commodity to be bought and sold, he claimed. We should not be overly concerned about traceability, as this was not how the gold supply chain worked. What we should be promoting was a mass balancing scheme; mass balancing would allow us to mix Fairtrade gold with gold from other sources and still certify it as Fairtrade. At worst it would allow you to buy a kilo of gold from any source you liked – such as a bank or refiner where the provenance of the gold was unknowable – pay a premium directly to the certified mining group, so the premium was paid, but the gold you actually called Fairtrade did not come from the certified source itself. This meant the consumer would have no guarantees that the gold they were buying was Fairtrade or dirty gold. To me, this dilution or mass balancing would mislead consumers. For the gold trader, this was the most effective model of business, taking small profits on large volumes traded. Traceability meant extra costs and fewer profits, and effectively curbed the position of the trader in the supply chain.

The ARM gold trader's anxiety was understandable. Would going Fairtrade remove the need for traders in the supply chain altogether? Within the Fairtrade system everyone – traders, manufacturers, and jewellers – would have access to the miners directly. The system would be more transparent. To be fair to him, he made a very good point regarding volumes. We needed a Fairtrade gold system that could be scaled up to get volumes to drive benefits to the miners, and on this point everyone agreed.

But I found myself being painted into a corner, viewed unfairly as someone who stood against volume and was only interested in small volumes of gold that had a high value.

My position was clear. Fairtrade gold did not mean a volume versus value market; it was both. But like all new Fairtrade products, the sales would start slowly and in relatively low volumes, and would build over time in a sustainable fashion. What we needed to do was focus on gradually building a sustainable market share. The conversion of consumers to Fairtrade gold would not happen overnight. We would need patience and unity among ourselves, as well as with FLO.

Gold traders are not consumer-facing; they are middlemen who do not interact with customer aspirations and as such have no experience of how to handle consumer expectations. If we launched an untraceable supply chain of gold, we would quite rightly have the campaign groups, consumers, and customers crawling all over us for deceiving the market. Fairtrade gold would be dead in the water at launch. For years FLO had interacted with customers on the issue of traceability in other Fairtrade supply chains, and any loss of traceability was always a big point of sensitivity with consumers.

They also had their reputation to preserve. For a luxury consumer product such as gold, with such a globally corrupt supply chain, it was even more important for us to be as squeaky clean as possible. The Fairtrade gold that ended up in the wedding ring of the customer had to be the gold that came from a certified Fairtrade gold mine. To me it was common sense.

The difficulties inside the organization increased again when ARM took the decision to create its own consumer label. I argued strongly that ARM did not need a label, as it was a group that worked with miners, not consumers. It simply did not have the capacity to manage an international consumer label and all the additional pressures and financial costs this would bring. It was tough enough working with miners, never mind managing a consumer brand as well. This was in essence why we needed the partnership with FLO. ARM would concentrate on working with miners, FLO would concentrate on developing the business customers. But again we found ourselves conflating and confusing an issue around our institutional profile with consumers, while our primary role was as a producer-support organization.

In my opinion, for us to build a strong, sustainable long-term Fairtrade gold market for the miners, we needed a simple market narrative. Fairtrade gold was a short, simple, memorable, and understandable proposition. To add anything to it would confuse the customer and detract from our potential to get market penetration.

ARM began to behave as if it had the right to dictate what the market was going to look like, because it claimed they had done the majority of work toward creating the Fairtrade and Fairmined gold standard (in this process Cristina had been exemplary). However, this was not completely true. ARM had copied the Fairtrade framework for standards creation and then populated that generic framework with specific issues relevant to small-scale miners. Also, ARM had been funded by international organizations and had solicited the help of specific technical experts in cyanide management and mercury usage, mining consultants and input from groups like the International Labour Organization, as well as members from FLO's own standards unit.

The culmination of this work was the creation of the Fairtrade and Fairmined gold standard that was in fact a wonderful example of the international community coming together to create this groundbreaking document. But now certain people on the ARM board were talking about owning the Fairtrade gold standard, and of needing to have a consumer label so customers would know about the institution of ARM. I found the whole affair deeply frustrating.

Here we had a group of people who had never sold a piece of jewellery in their lives, who now saw themselves as experts in marketing jewellery, prescribing solutions about labelling that would ultimately be counterproductive. For years I had been in discussions with the jewellery industry, big and small, and the one unanimous factor in every discussion was: "We want the Fairtrade mark; that's where the value lies for us." The ARM Fairmined label looked OK on a piece of paper, but in practice it would simply confuse the customer, make trading in Fairtrade gold more expensive for the licence holders, and be counterproductive to ARM's stated objective of securing large volume sales of gold for the miners.

I also knew from the many years I had stood behind the counter in the jewellery shop that consumers would not accept mass balancing in gold on a Fairtrade labelled piece of jewellery. The only way mass balancing could work is if you decoupled the supply chain from the labelled consumer product, and if we did that, how would anyone know that what they were buying was from a Fairtrade certified source? We had to ensure that any product that was labelled and stamped as Fairtrade gold was traceable back to the certified mine. It was matter of product integrity and basic honesty.

Every board meeting, we had to go through this debate, and I finally lost my temper, jumping to my feet, slamming my fist down on the table, and shouting, "I will not let you lie to the consumers. It is wrong."

Although I may not have covered myself in glory at that precise moment, the overt show of raw emotion was one I was not sorry for. Better to have passion and belief than bland and insipid theories that manifest themselves in the constant politics of the corridor. I believe in transparency, emotions and all.

I was definitely now in the minority on the board and I sensed that with the proposed change in the chair it would only be a matter of time before ARM went the corporate institutional way and migrated toward groups such as the Responsible Jewellery Council. RJC at the time had no desire to promote traceability in the gold supply chain.

Michael Rae, the ex-World Wildlife Fund Australia man who was now the CEO of RJC, was categorical in a Fair Jewellery Action-published interview[2] I had with him, in which he said the RJC was not going to do any work on what they called "chain of custody". It was too complicated to reorganize the big mining companies and the refiners so they were traceable. But I was not going to give up on the basic principles of transparency and traceability in the gold supply chain. I had to stay in my role as vice-chair of ARM until we had successfully negotiated the partnership with FLO and had a signed piece of paper. Once both groups had signed, I would resign.

Catalina's announcement that she was stepping down as chair meant we needed to restructure the negotiation team that was creating the partnership with FLO, and because I had the strongest relationship with FLO, I became the second part of the team to lead the negotiations through to contract.

Negotiations had started well, building on the outline of the MoU that both parties had signed following Chris Davis's trip to Peru in 2007. Over nearly eighteen months I shuttled between London, Bonn, and Colombia, attending pre-negotiation and negotiation meetings, and ARM board meetings where the details of the partnership contract were discussed in detail. The issues that going into partnership with FLO presented to ARM were:

- governance and management of the project
- the use of income and royalties on gold sales and who would get that income
- the labelling of the gold to the consumer
- the ownership of the Fairtrade Fairmined standard
- the termination and penalties in the event of a breach of contract
- how we would review the partnership at the end of the contract.

We worked tirelessly as a team to get the best deal for small-scale miners, and by the time we turned up to our final scheduled negotiation meeting on 9 October 2009, we had agreed 90 per cent of what would become the partnership between the two organizations. FLO had given ground on the key issue of ownership of the gold standard with a settlement that it would go into public ownership at the end of the three-year partnership. It seemed a fair compromise and also appeared to have satisfied ARM's need for recognition of the hard work they had put into its creation.

However, as we sat in the meeting with our FLO counterparts, it became apparent that all was not well. The other member of our negotiation team was aggressive and seemed determined to revisit issues we had already agreed, such as termination clauses and how ARM would be communicated to the world through press statements. I was reeling. We had covered all these issues over the last twelve months and now ARM appeared to be opening up old debates and representing them as obstacles to closure.

FLO made some very good points. No organization can manage what the press reports or how they frame it. The likelihood would be that the language of Fairtrade would be the dominant language, as the Fairtrade mark was what consumers and the press understood. However frustrating that might be to ARM, it was just a reality and there was very little anyone could do about it. What we could control was the nomenclature in our joint press releases, and on that point FLO and ARM would always be mentioned together.

For my ARM counterpart this was not acceptable. She exploded and began shouting one of the FLO team down. I couldn't believe it. The lady from FLO put out the fire by saying she did not appreciate being shouted at by people who were supposed to be partners. It was deeply embarrassing and we clearly needed a break for lunch.

After lunch we continued in much the same vein, going around in circles. With everything we discussed, my counterpart presented a problem as to why we could not go forward. We were sitting around a table representing the collective hopes and dreams of miners and jewellers, and the goodwill of all the ARM donors, as well as FLO staff and supporters who were very excited about the idea of Fairtrade gold. We had over sixty-one companies in the UK, plus Finnish, Dutch, Canadian, American, French, Swedish, and German jewellers, all of whom had expressed a clear desire to use certified gold. We had signed off the now Fairtrade Fairmined gold and associated precious metals standard through the joint standards committee.

For all of us, the project we had been working on since Peru in 2006 was in jeopardy because one person could not close the deal. Simply put, my counterpart did not trust FLO and was not prepared to conclude the deal. Eventually I called a stop to what was now a serious embarrassment for ARM.

I was furious. It seemed as though my counterpart was playing a game of deliberate brinkmanship with our future partners and had become angry when she could not get her way. As we said our goodbyes, I was sure that as a result of these outbursts of unprofessional behaviour, FLO would not want to work with us, as ARM would be seen as a liability.

As we both walked down the grey Bonn streets, we found a small café, I ordered a coffee, and we sat in silence. I thought, given the seriousness of what had just taken place, my best bet was to hold my tongue, for fear of another public tantrum from my colleague. Once my ARM colleague realized I was in no mood for talking, she walked off back to the hotel leaving me to my own thoughts and an espresso coffee. What should I do? I was concerned for ARM's reputation.

It felt like I faced Hobson's choice. I could start ringing around the ARM team and highlight what had happened and, in doing so, begin a war within the organization, or I could walk back to the FLO office and apologize directly to FLO on behalf of ARM and seek to redeem some of our lost credibility.

I decided to apologize. The FLO team were very understanding. They graciously accepted the apology and reassured me that they would be willing to talk further, once ARM had resolved exactly how it wanted to proceed. I found the whole situation truly paradoxical. However, despite an accepted apology, I was not sure what damage this would do to ARM's internal relationships. Would ARM harden to save institutional face, and decide to pull out of the partnership altogether?

I called Catalina, explained what had occurred, and that I was due to travel to India the following day. I would get my report on what had happened in the meeting to her on my return, in time for our scheduled board meeting on 25 November, where we were due to vote on ratifying the partnership.

As I wandered through the drab streets of Bonn back to my hotel, I called Ruth at home. For a number of years we'd had a bottle of champagne in the fridge that was set aside for the day that Fairtrade gold was launched to the international market. I was heartbroken and had resigned myself to the fact that we had failed at the last hurdle. I was utterly gutted. Tears welled up in my eyes as I told Ruth to take the bottle out the fridge, as we would not need it. Ruth's reply was the tonic I needed.

"No! You have not come this far and fought this hard to give up now!"

CHAPTER ELEVEN

We now have the best gold story in the world.

On 25 November 2009, the Alliance for Responsible Mining voted to approve the three-year partnership with FLO. It was a huge relief to everyone. Since the episode in Bonn, phones had been ringing non-stop as we worked tirelessly to rescue and finalize the partnership agreement.

As with any negotiation, there were two elements – the legal work undertaken by lawyers, and the relational investment into the people who ultimately will be your partners. I was less concerned about the legal document, as it would not be worth the ink if both parties did not trust one another. Chris Davis from Fairtrade and I spent hours ironing out the consequences of the relational fallout. I talked a few weeks after the Bonn event with my counterpart in the negotiation team and agreed a way we could work together to complete the deal. We agreed to disagree on whether FLO were the best labelling partners for gold and decided that ultimately the board of ARM would choose whether to sign the three year partnership deal.

Once we re-engaged with FLO, it became a matter of when we signed, not if we were going to sign. The principle objections that ARM had to the partnership were now dealt with, the institutional ego had considerably diminished since the infamous outburst, and ARM weighed up the pros and cons of signing. The general consensus was that we had all travelled too far over the last five years to throw it all away. The yes votes outnumbered the two no votes and the contract was ratified. I was relieved that common sense had prevailed. All that remained now was for FLO to approve the deal at their own board meeting, which they dutifully did on 8 December.

We had done it. The partnership was signed and sealed. All that remained now was to prepare the market and get the miners ready to be certified. I informed ARM I would be resigning. I was hugely relieved when I left ARM, as the politics in the organization were exhausting. What had started out as a grass roots organization was rapidly turning into a top-down politically motivated group. I had no appetite to be a part of an organization that, in my opinion, seemed more concerned with preserving its own institution than it was in serving the small-scale miners.

The year 2009 had been a monumental one for me. Apart from the tricky and at times explosive negotiations with ARM and FLO and the challenges in Greenland with the ruby miners, I had also decided it was time to leave CRED Jewellery. My reasons were complex and it was a very difficult decision, as I loved the company. There was no doubt in my mind we were the best ethical jeweller in the market. CRED had become the vehicle through which I had engaged a secretive and often corrupt industry, and demonstrated that consumers wanted an ethical jewellery product when they were presented with it. The lessons CRED Jewellery had learned along the way were invaluable, and the people and places we were now working with were beyond my wildest dreams. CRED had established itself as a trusted source when it came to ethical jewellery. It was no small achievement for a small company.

When we embarked on the journey to deliver ethical fair trade jewellery following that very first trip to India, I had set an internal goal in our Chichester store to be the first jeweller in the world to be 100 per cent traceable from mine to retail on all of our products. It was a tongue-in-cheek goal that I was never sure we would be able to fulfil.

At the time, we could not run a jewellery business 100 per cent traceable on all our lines, but we could at least start the transition toward that objective and see how long it would take us to achieve that. The work alongside Oro Verdé and ARM, and lessons learned in Greenland, Peru, Tanzania, and Sierra Leone, had all contributed to our knowledge base, from both a human rights and an environmental perspective, and we had integrated these values into a traceable ethic for our jewellery. We knew how to deliver jewellery with soul and intelligence.

But increasingly I came to realize that I had taken the company as far as I could and this was not an easy thing to come to terms with. A part of my ego dictated I stay on and pretend I could make the business side of it work, but I was in heart and essence a campaigner and social entrepreneur. What CRED now needed was a businessperson who could apply some of the bottom line disciplines every business needs in order to succeed commercially. It needed someone who would build upon the ethical foundations and knowledge base that had been created.

It was obvious to everyone within the company that my role in the industry had changed. I was now more identified with the issues the jewellery trade faced, and more especially to the campaign on Fairtrade gold. I felt confident that the existing team in CRED could cope without me, had the knowledge to take the company forward, and could manage the complexities of the supply chains we had created. So in September 2009 I stepped aside from being a director and handed over to Andrew Hunter and Christian Cheesman.

But what I was not so sure about was the Fairtrade Foundation's ability to deliver this Fairtrade gold idea to an idiosyncratic and deeply secretive jewellery industry. There were also people within Fairtrade who shared the same concerns and, once my resignations from CRED and ARM were public, they approached me to work with them over 2010 to prepare the jewellery trade in the UK for the launch of certified Fairtrade gold. This would not be easy, despite the top line rhetoric within the industry of being supportive to the idea. Beneath the surface there remained the conservative reticence and lingering nervousness to the idea of Fairtrade and the extra costs involved. This could be highlighted by three incidents that occurred in late 2008 and 2009.

Gordon Hamme, then editor of *The Goldsmith Magazine*, had for a long time been a vocal and public detractor of the idea of Fairtrade gold. His credentials in the industry went back a long way and his knowledge of gold trading was extensive, as he had built up and then sold his jewellery supply company to the country's largest jewellery supplier, Cookson's. Gordon just could not or would not believe that fair trade was possible in gold. It was simply too complicated a supply chain to prove traceability, never mind certify it. How could Fairtrade guarantee that the miners would not just top up their production from non-fair trade sources and claim the Fairtrade premium for gold from a non-fair trade source? This was a very real challenge to the integrity of the Fairtrade claim, and one that no one in the system could ignore.

Gordon was typical of the dissenting voice of the industry. We would cross swords at the now obligatory ethical debates that took place at the national trade shows in London and Birmingham. It was always a cordial showdown, but underneath the civility there was the very real issue of change, accountability, and the status quo.

When the press releases came out announcing the launch of the Fairtrade gold standard, the partnership agreement between FLO and ARM, and the countdown to market launch, Gordon, Ute Decker, a fantastic German ethical sculptural jeweller working out of London, and I met in Maxwell's burger restaurant in Covent Garden in London.

"Valerio, you're the most dangerous bastard in our industry," Gordon proclaimed, as he finally conceded that we were going to do it. I had always seen Gordon as a cynic, but he proved me wrong and his magnanimous confession encouraged me that we might finally be breaking through the hard-core opposition to Fairtrade gold.

The second challenge we faced was highlighted through ongoing meetings I was having with some of the UK and European jewellery brands. Since 2007 I had been talking to Beaverbrooks about the possibility of them becoming a future user of Fairtrade gold. The conversation had been a very positive one and their then CEO, Mark Addlestone, had long been a supporter of ethical improvements in the jewellery industry. Mark had been the voice of support when I first gave my "Towards an Ethical Jewellery Business" presentation to the National Association of Goldsmiths in 2003.

Beaverbrooks invited me to visit their HQ in Lancashire, where we discussed at length the challenges that jewellers would face in selling a gold product that carried a premium price. Beaverbrooks's biggest anxiety at the meeting was that if they sold Fairtrade gold, what would it say about their other products that were not Fairtrade? Would customers be turned off buying their jewellery if they knew not all jewellery was fair or sourced well? This anxiety was an understandable one that always cropped up when a new Fairtrade product came on the market, and in almost every case consumers reacted in exactly the opposite way, praising the retailer for doing the best they could with what was available.

Kalevala Jewelry is based in Helsinki, and they flew me to Finland to meet with their management team, to tour their excellent manufacturing base, and to explore how they could integrate Fairtrade principles into their jewellery production. It was clear from the outset that Kalevala were no ordinary jewellery brand. For a start, their ownership structure was entirely made up of women, genuinely refreshing in an industry that at board level is still male dominated. Equally, their desire to integrate

Fairtrade into their jewellery would be made easier as they did not outsource their manufacturing. They would be able to track and trace the Fairtrade gold right through their system, an essential part of maintaining the trust of the consumer when you claim Fairtrade status on your collections.

What was going to prove difficult for them was the Fairtrade premium, and they rightly wanted to understand how you can stop premium costs escalating through the pricing structure, causing the jewellery to be way too expensive.

These were examples of some of the marketing and financial challenges that Fairtrade would have to deal with, and although not very exciting to talk about publicly, they would have to be answered if we were going to persuade the jewellery industry to move from intellectual support of the idea to using Fairtrade gold in jewellery-making. Clearly persuading jewellery companies that paying a Fairtrade premium on their gold was not going to ruin their finances was going to be as big a challenge as getting the miners certified.

FLO did not have any experience in working with a non-agricultural product such as gold, or working within the jewellery profession. This in itself would be a mountain for them to climb.

When I began my work with them, I started by taking the staff that had been assigned to the gold project to the Royal Exchange opposite the Bank of England in the City of London. Here in this old classically styled market exchange building was now a fine set of restaurants and wine bars serving the City elite. On the ground floor was a concentrated mass of luxury jewellery brands such as the LVMH-owned De Beers diamond jewellery brand, Cartier, Boodles, Theo Fennell, Tiffany, and Bulgari. I wanted them to understand the aspirational and emotional element that is central to the jewellery sale.

I had asked Tom, the manager of Boodles, if he would spend some time with the Fairtrade women and explain to them what a premium jewellery customer expected. He produced a marquise-cut yellow diamond and platinum cocktail ring valued at £180,000 and asked them to try it on.

"How does that make you feel?" he asked.

The responses summed up jewellery. One of the women, normally a fairly hard-nosed career type, was speechless and eventually, when she found her tongue, explained she felt like a princess and special. Another of the women wouldn't touch it out of protest at its extravagance, while another exclaimed that this was the price of her one-bedroom flat.

Tom was great with them. Jewellery is all about the emotion it conjures up in people; it's about making you feel a million dollars, unique, and exclusive. It is about creating memories and stories.

As we sat in his store, drinking sparkling water and white wine, the Fairtrade staff began to understand that when a customer buys jewellery, they don't just pick it off the shelf like tea or coffee. They spend time on the sale; the romance is key, the emotional connection and memory associated with the purchase is exclusive to them, as any newly engaged couple will testify.

Jewellery is talismanic. For a jeweller, a good customer comes back three, maybe four times a year, as opposed to the weekly shop at Tesco or Sainsbury's. How we presented Fairtrade gold to the market would be crucial. Here was an opportunity to present the Fairtrade movement as coming of age, as it was now embracing a luxury, high-value commodity such as gold and redirecting more of that luxury value back to the poor.

I had first met Michael Allchin, the chief executive and Assay Master of the Birmingham Assay Office at the Cape Town talk I had given. He was a supporter of the idea of Fairtrade gold and offered the help of the Assay Office when it was needed. Now the guys at Fairtrade had set an initial launch date of November 2010, we needed his help in two ways. Would he work with Fairtrade on creating a special stamp, similar to a hallmark, which could be used on every piece of Fairtrade gold jewellery that came to the market, so the consumer would know that the gold they were wearing was from a Fairtrade source? And also, would he host a meeting at the Assay Office in Birmingham with all the key jewellery moguls – refiners, gold bullion dealers, gold traders, jewellery manufacturers, and some of the multiple high street retail jewellers?

It is always fascinating and entertaining to sit in the same room as industry competitors. Testosterone often impregnates every comment and, when coupled with historical business fallouts, it was amazing that Michael had managed to get so many people together, a testimony to the levels of interest that were now being generated about this product called Fairtrade gold.

The "peacocking" throughout that summer's day in 2010 culminated in the owner of one of the UK's biggest gold bullion and jewellery supply dealers declaring: "Fairtrade gold is a dreadful idea. It will ruin our industry and I am happy to buy up all the production just to keep it off the market."

He was unlikely to join the scheme, but it did allow Fairtrade to present the social and environmental justification for why Fairtrade and ARM were launching Fairtrade gold. This became the typical sort of meeting that Victoria Waugh, the Fairtrade commercial manager for gold, and I would spend much of the summer attending, as we travelled around the UK recruiting industry players to sign up to the launch and commit to using and supplying Fairtrade gold.

By the end of that summer, we had over twenty-five retail jewellers, plus other industry actors that we required to support a commercial launch, and I was very proud as CRED Jewellery were first in the queue. I found it remarkable that we had assembled some of the great and the good in the industry to back the plan. Not only did we have the intentional ethical jewellers such as Vivien Johnston, April Doubleday, Ingle & Rhode, Oria Jewellery, and Ute Decker, but we were also attracting the likes of Pippa Small, Stephen Webster, Stephen Einhorn, Jacqueline Rabun, and Harriet Kelsall.

My only disappointment was that despite talking to brands such as Cartier, Tiffany, and Boodles, none of them were prepared to come on board for the launch. It would have cost them very little in real terms and would have demonstrated a commitment to human rights and environmental responsibility. But I should not have been surprised, as according to the "Uplifting the Earth"[1] report Fair Jewellery Action had co-published with Lifeworth,[2] some of the world's leading jewellery brands including Boucheron, Buccellati, Bulgari, Chanel, Chopard, Graff Diamonds, Harry Winston, and Van Cleef & Arpels were next to useless when it came to ethical issues. It concluded that the major reason for their poor ethical performance was "inadequate focus on traceability and pro-poor development issues, insufficient transparency, the emphasis on safety rather than opportunity and limited attention to relationships". It went on to comment that "Information on social and environmental performance is difficult to obtain from luxury jewellery companies, indicating a general lack of transparency". I reassured myself that real change never comes from the big boys; it always starts with the little people.

Having campaigned for so long to achieve this, there remained niggling doubts in my mind that it was going to happen and I had to pinch myself on a regular basis as we inched closer week by week to the official launch. We were genuinely seeing a cultural shift in the UK jewellery industry. Yet despite the progress we were making with the retailers and industry players, there were still doubts that the miners would be ready to sell to market for the agreed launch date. There seemed to be problems on the ground in Colombia with Oro Verdé and also with Cotapata, a co-op from Bolivia.

In Colombia the certifiers had done their job thoroughly and had uncovered that not all the green gold miners had registered properly with Oro Verdé. On one level it was a technicality. But given the risks associated with the selling of non-Fairtrade gold into the system (frequently highlighted by sceptics such as Gordon Hamme), there was absolutely no way the independent certifier could allow Oro Verdé to sell without all the proper registrations in place.

This was bitterly disappointing for them and me, as Oro Verdé had been the first set of artisanal miners to pioneer eco-mining and had laid the foundations for the Fairtrade opportunity in gold. I had wanted them to be the first to deliver Fairtrade gold to market, but this delay would mean it was certain they would not manage this, as re-registering everyone in their system would take a few months, given the remote jungle locations some of the miners lived in. But it also demonstrated the strength of having the independent certifiers FLO-Cert, who, despite knowing about all the expectations surrounding the world's first Fairtrade gold, did their job in highlighting the discrepancy, and made Oro Verdé go back and get it right. This to me was vindication that the system worked and could be trusted by the jewellers as well as consumers.

Cotapata on the other hand were having a different sort of registration challenge. The Bolivian government insisted on charging 7 per cent tax on gold exports for companies. If you registered as a co-op, it was only 2.5 per cent. Not all the documents were up to date and this meant going back and refiling the correct paperwork. This was purely a clerical issue that was swiftly resolved, but not quite in time for the proposed market launch in November.

So we took the decision to postpone till February 2011. Needless to say the jewellers were disappointed, and some disgruntled. They, alongside the traders, manufacturers, and jewellery suppliers had been busy registering within the Fairtrade system, and gearing up for November with product and publicity. It meant massive frustration for everyone but at least we could give them a new date, Valentine's Day 2011. But would Cotapata and Oro Verdé be ready in time? We would find out in January.

As January arrived, I was a ball of nervous energy. The UK jewellery industry was ready to pop in anticipation; my phone was as hot as the devil's lead pencil with the press wanting endless interviews. The excitement in the industry was unprecedented. A bonus for us was the Canadians had decided to launch Fairtrade gold at the same time as the UK, so we now had two countries launching simultaneously. But we still did not know if Oro Verdé and Cotapata would be ready for the new launch date. When Gemma Cartwright, the gold project manager at Fairtrade, finally announced that Cotapata had been certified and would have a kilo bar ready for launch, everyone in Fairtrade and ARM and the jewellers breathed a huge sigh of relief. At home I wept as all the emotion and expectation came pouring out. We would do it. All that remained now was for Fairtrade to put the launch event together, not something I was required to be involved in. But before I could get to launch, I had one more international trip to do: Sierra Leone.

Ever since 2005 and my first visit to Sierra Leone I had wanted to travel back there and explore the gold mines, and if possible begin to build some relationships in Africa similar to the one that I had built with Oro Verdé. My first love has always been Africa, and despite my wonderful experiences in South America, my aching desire had always been to see African miners benefit from the developmental potential in the Fairtrade gold idea. So when Brima Conteh, a Sierra Leonean activist and founder of Diaspora Afrique (an orgnization dedicated to promoting positive relations between people of African descent living in Europe and the home countries from which they originally came) invited me to visit some of the chiefdoms around the town of Makeni, it was too good an opportunity to turn down.

It was a beautiful trip. Sierra Leone had become the country known for the fighting over its minerals because of the brutal and savage rebel insurgency that had been paid for through its diamonds. This war had irrevocably changed the jewellery industry with the introduction of the Kimberley Process, created to stop the flow of blood diamonds entering the jewellery supply chain. But it seemed unfair that Sierra Leone should be famous for this, in the same way as Ethiopia is always viewed through the lens of famine.

In preparation for our trip, a friend of mine, Alex Hamilton, had organized half a tonne of clothes and educational materials from local schools and churches to be sent to the paramount chief of Sambaia Chiefdom as a goodwill gesture.

By the time we arrived in the tiny chief village of Sambaia, it was the dead of night. There was no electricity in the village, and the stars hung low and big in the sky with a wonderful crescent moon smiling down. The villagers had been waiting for us to arrive all day, and as we climbed out of the 4x4 and eased our bodies into a standing position, the drums started and three men in traditional costume performed some eccentric magic tricks and sword-swallowing routines for us by way of a ceremonial greeting. That night I slept soundly on top of a huge pile of grain sacks in the paramount chief's house, with only the tiny munching of grain mites for company.

In the cool light of the following morning, I began to understand the nature of the heavy rural poverty that exists in the bush of Sierra Leone. This was clearly going to be a hard trip, travelling around the rural gold fields of three of the principal gold-producing chiefdoms, Sambaia, Diang, and Sanda Loko. But before we could get out on the road, we had to attend the handing-over ceremony that the paramount chief had called to receive our gifts of clothes and educational materials for the local schools. Both Alex and I were totally unaware that it was a traditional act to offer a gift when entering into a new chiefdom. Normally this offering would be kola nuts or money, so our shipment had rather exceeded the normal greeting gift. The community were so touched they had erupted with joy when the shipment arrived and wanted to honour us for the gifts.

In a ceremony that lasted over an hour, I was made a ceremonial paramount chief and given the name Alhaji Kolio

Jalloh I, meaning "The First Godly Holy Tribal Warrior". Alex was anointed as Chief Fabolo Kenfa Jalloh, meaning "Chief Tribal Hunter", which was pretty good for an ex-marine. In short, we were given the freedom of the chiefdom, and we were both acutely aware what an honour it was to have been received so graciously into the heart of it.

As we hit the road, our first visit was to a small village that had no proper school or church. I was deeply impressed that the Muslim majority in this region was concerned that the Christian minority lacked a place of worship and were keen to impress this fact upon us. As we finished looking at what was not much more than a few simple dwellings made from mud and palm leaf roofing that acted as the village school, a tiny old man came up to me, shoved his prosthetic limb into my hand, and shook it firmly. He looked at me intently for a few seconds as if weighing up my soul for judgment and said, "I lost my arm in the war; the rebels cut it off. Will you please make sure that my grandchildren have an education so that we will never have war again in our country?"

The weight of these words and the moral clarity of such simple requests have always carried the presence of God for me, and I was stuck for words. How do you reply to such a honest request? I could not answer yes: that would be a lie, as I was not in a position to offer a hope I could not fulfil. Nor could I fob the man off, so we talked about our lives, family, and children, and I listened to his horrific story and told him that all I could do was try. Climbing into the 4x4 to head off to the mines made me realize how fragile the relationship between life, death, and conflict minerals is in this crazy world of poverty, small-scale mining, and jewellery.

At that point, all the small-scale mining sites I had seen had been places of expansive wilderness, remote and harsh, with small communities of hundreds, sometimes thousands grinding out a basic living from the minerals of the earth. As I stepped out of a small river valley that led down to Lake Sonfon, what I witnessed was on a scale I had never imagined.

Here were tens of thousands of bodies, lined up in chain gangs, carving cubist-style terraces out of the land on both sides of the valley. At the foot of each set of terraces were teams of diggers standing up to their waists in mud, shovelling the earth into round pans that were then thrown upward through the hands of the chain gang that numbered anywhere up to twenty or thirty people, until it got to the top of the hill.

Everywhere was thick with noise. Smoke filled the air from the tiny opportunistic food stalls that had been set up to feed the workers. The river that had originally created what must have been a beautiful valley just disappeared into mud. Children were everywhere, including the mine pits. It was an apocalyptic scene of devastation on a scale I could not take in. In every way I was emotionally, spiritually, and visually overwhelmed, and all I could do was stand in silence and allow the vision before me to burn itself into my consciousness.

The journey to the next town where we were due to meet the Speaker, who is the deputy to the paramount chief of Diang Chiefdom, was a silent one for me. Once inside his small house, we talked the ceremonial small talk and finally got down to business. I asked questions about Lake Sonfon and found out that this site was actually owned by the Speaker himself. Every worker on that site delivered the gold to him. They were all paid a dollar a day plus a meal. My head count turned out to be right as there were in excess of 10,000 workers on that site. The Speaker seemed pleased I was taking such an interest in his operation and offered to show us other equally large mining sites in the area. He boasted that every month he made $100,000 of profit on the gold he sold to American and Ukrainian buyers. I declined his offer and got up to leave.

As the others concluded the formalities, I paced outside his house to cool my festering anger. A small girl not much older than nine came up to me, and out of her dress pocket produced a foil lining from a cigarette box that she unfolded to reveal a few grams of gold. She asked if I would like to buy it. I asked her where she got the gold and she explained her mother ran the little tea and coffee booth opposite the Speaker's house. This is how her family made a living, by serving the Speaker. She obtained her gold as every month, when the foreigners came to the Speaker's house, they always brought a huge crate of beer with them and when the gold had been sold and the money had changed hands, they would all get drunk. She would then sit under the trading table and wait for the drunken men to spill some of the gold onto the ground. She would collect it and sell it to others to top up her family income.

Here in this small village, without a school, health clinic, electricity, or decent sanitation, the gold crumbs from the tables of injustice were being used by the innocent to meet their daily needs. It brought a whole new understanding to the phrase "make friends with unrighteous Mammon".

Fairtrade gold from Africa was going to be a completely different challenge from the one faced in South America.

Landing back in the UK, I was not afforded my usual few days off to acclimatize back to home life. The Fairtrade gold launch was only a few weeks away and I was back to the press bandwagon. The national broadsheets, tabloids, online blogs, industry press, and radio were all queuing up to talk. I began to taste a little of what it must be like if you are a celebrity, with the constant pressure to comment, explain, and answer for your every move.

The launch event itself I remember very little of. I climbed off the Tube at Farringdon station and walked up Greville Street and into The Hatton Conference Centre on Hatton Garden. I walked slowly as I was apprehensive, a bag of contradictory emotions.

My mind raced through the story from the first time Ethiopian customs confiscated my jewellery purchases to the garnet mine in Rajasthan and the anger I felt at these events. I recalled the scepticism and silence I got from the industry when I first started talking about the idea of fair trade in the jewellery industry, and the frustration of being ignored. I thought of my first meeting with Catalina in London and the Colombian trip to visit the Oro Verdé miners who were as excited as I was at finding someone who believed in the same traceability values as they did; meeting Marc Choyt, a man as passionate about honesty and transparency in the jewellery trade as I was; starting Fair Jewellery Action and working with the people of Greenland on the ruby rights campaign.

I was also apprehensive and very sad that the relationship with ARM had turned out so negatively. I was not looking forward to seeing them again. Yet despite our personal differences, the very Fairtrade gold reality would not have happened without them. They were a vital part of making it a reality. Chance meetings with Harriet Lamb at Katharine Hamnett's house, children working with mercury in Peru, endless boring but essential Fairtrade gold standards meetings, the smiles and courage of the small-scale miners, and the recent scenes I had witnessed in Sierra Leone: all these stories and many others came flooding back to me.

As I entered The Hatton Conference Centre, the first person I saw was the tall and imposing Alan Frampton, the new owner of CRED Jewellery. As the apprehension faded away, I remembered Anita Roddick's words to me: "Greg, just tell the story." And that is what I did.

In my pocket I had ten grams of Oro Verdé gold given to me by CRED Jewellery and I had decided to give it to the Fairtrade Foundation as a thank you for their commitment to making Fairtrade gold a reality. With Harriet's introduction followed by Cristina Echavarria's presentation on behalf of ARM, I got up to address the room full of media, jewellers, activists, and all those who had worked tirelessly to create this groundbreaking product.

We had done it and I was extremely proud of our success. I thanked ARM for their phenomenal efforts in securing the standards, and turned to give Harriet the small gold grains from Oro Verdé as a symbol of my appreciation for the sacrifices she personally, as well as the organization, had made to bring this dream to a successful market launch. For me it felt like I had already run the marathon and reached the finishing line, but my closing comments to the group assembled pointed out

> *the jewellery industry and society has treated gold like an emasculated commodity; what we have done here with Fairtrade is put the soul back into gold; we have given it a personality, given it life, given it an origin, given it a customer, and, most of all, given it a voice. The power to change this industry rests not in the money alone; it also rests in the story and we now have the best gold story in the world. In reality, getting to the launch of Fairtrade gold means we have arrived at the start of the race. Welcome to the start of the journey.*

But the final and most powerful moment had been saved for Juana Peña Endora, the leader of the Bolivian small-scale gold mining cooperative, Cotapata. Juana represented everything we had fought to achieve and as she stood up to address the audience, this timid-looking lady opened a leather box and pulled out the first ever 1 kilo bar of certified Fairtrade gold to show to the waiting press. As she stood over it, with cameras clicking, tears of joy fell from her eyes onto the purest bar of gold in the world. It was a moment I shall never forget.

EPILOGUE

January 2013

The light... is near to the darkness.

The book of Job[1]

Anyone who travels in Africa must be blessed with patience and an unswerving belief in the inherent goodness of humanity, not something I believe St Augustine (an African himself), the "inventor" of the doctrine of original sin, had in abundance when he came up with that innately negative outlook. This belief was tested upon my arrival at Entebbe Airport, where I was transiting to Bunia in the Eastern Democratic Republic of the Congo (DRC).

The immigration officer retains my passport and allows me the freedom of this singularly underwhelming airport. I then wait four hours for what is increasingly looking like a mythical representative of the small airline company who will be flying me to Bunia to issue me with my pre-paid ticket. As I sit in almost complete solitude, I have reoccurring visions of scenes of torture and abuse from the film *The Last King of Scotland*, grateful those days of Idi Amin have long disappeared from Uganda.

Eventually a lady arrives from the airline company and asks for my passport. For ten heart-stopping minutes the half dozen immigration officials, who are all busy chatting, half-heartedly move piles of envelopes and papers from one side of their desks to the other, while telling me I need to relax. In this matter of humanity's inherent goodness I am vindicated as my passport turns up from another room, only to disappear again with the airline lady to be shown to another mythological person in an upstairs room.

After another two hours the small twin prop flight to Bunia dances through the clouds and over a scattering of lakes, rocky hills, bush, and forest that keeps my aching body entertained. Bush fire smoke drifts across the landscape telling us the wind direction and that the land beneath is inhabited by, if you believe the popular media myths of the West, bandits, militia, and smugglers of conflict gold; a narrative I have been guilty of perpetuating in my career as an ethical jewellery campaigner, and not without a measure of truth attached to it.

Arriving at the Bunia airstrip is a small education in the challenges the DRC faces on a daily basis. After my passport is stamped with a date stamp similar to the ones you can buy in any stationery store, I collect my bag from the nose of the plane and take it to a room full of cardboard boxes and plastic chairs to be inspected by a customs official in a garish blue and yellow shell suit. As he opens my bag he spots my camera and removes it from its box, and in an animated French Swahili diatribe, announces this is not permitted in the country. He declares it is a telescopic camera that can link to the Internet via a satellite and can also be used to film the local underwater wildlife that last appeared in this region during the Jurassic period.

Others begin to emerge from small rooms off the main cardboard box room and join in what rapidly conflates to a game of pass the parcel among eight grown men. Eventually the camera, in the mass confusion, disappears into a back room and I am told through Henri Ladyi, the coordinator of the Centre for Resolution Conflicts (CRC), that they want a $100 tax to import the camera. I refuse to pay.

As I am clearly no longer part of the discussion I decide to adopt a stance of calm self-preservation, as I recognize I am going to be here for a long time. I sit down, open my Bible, and go into a state of Zen-Christian Lectio Divina – the meditative practice of reading Scripture. Eventually the commotion attracts the attention of the airport police, and the situation becomes further magnified when the location of the camera cannot be determined. What had started as an attempt to bribe a visitor has now become a case of theft. Someone has stolen my camera.

The volume increases again to a pitch that would rival Jimi Hendrix's performance at the Isle of Wight Festival in 1970, as the airport customs boss now realizes that he has an incident on his hands that involves the police. With the head of airport police involved, the noise hits a new and more frenzied level. The customs officer in the garish shell suit has been found to have stashed the camera in his bag. He makes a statement to the police and after much to-ing and fro-ing between officials in the airport, the offender turns out to have been drinking and is now pleading to keep his job and not be charged with theft by the police.

The noise has by this stage reached the district head of customs, who has driven down to the airport to take personal control of what seems to have become a diplomatic incident. Three hours, two police statements, and a very contrite and worried corrupt customs official later, I am given back my camera by the district customs officer in a ceremony that includes a photo shoot, a very formal verbal apology, and a letter I have to sign absolving the authorities of all legal repercussions, all during a long and vigorous handshake. There is nothing low-key about my arrival.

Meeting Henri and hearing his story is very distressing as well as inspiring. It's distressing because he has suffered, like so many in this war-torn country. Having lost his father to a rebel attack, he joined a local militia in order to protect his family from other similar events. His story is inspirational because his wife persuaded him to turn from being militia to becoming a peacemaker when she threatened to pack up and leave for her parents'. The insecurity of living with violence was too much for her to cope with, especially with a young family.

In 2003, Henri and his family found themselves in the Mukulia Camp for Internally Displaced People as they fled the ethnic violence that had erupted at the time. While in the camp he started to work across the ethnic divides and to build a local peace movement by facilitating dialogue, interaction, and mutual understanding between historic rival groups.

I am to be based for the week in Bunia, one of the main towns in the Ituri district of Oriental province. Bunia is the home to the recently reopened United Nations peacekeeping mission. It had closed following an attack by students from the next-door university in an outpouring of anger and frustration at the unsettling and accidental death of a student at the hands of the UN. This student uprising forced the UN to move out of Bunia for a short period of time. It was a living testimony to the volatility of the region that a bunch of students could chase the UN out of town.

My first job is to register at the UN and to receive a security briefing. The guards seem slightly confused as I ask them where to go to register myself for security purposes. Eventually, after visiting three separate offices, I am introduced to a man who points to a map and informs me that the road is "green all the way to Aru in the north; anywhere south of Bogoro you will need a military escort and do not head west" (he points to a huge space on the map that is effectively empty) "as it is full of elephant poachers in helicopter gunships and militia". I am instructed to keep my satellite phone with me at all times and stay in radio contact. I am told as I leave that the current security situation is "calm but volatile".

I confess to being slightly nervous now as I do not have a satellite phone; all I have is a mobile phone signal and the wisdom of Henri and team who reassure me they know how to navigate this region with aplomb. Next we visit the Congolese security service office, where after an hour of French chit-chat, we are issued our travel stamp on the requisite document, I am given a lecture by the chief of security on why I should not be doing this, and we are sent on our way. My next stop is one of the artisanal mining sites that is part of the CRC peace-building process.

We live in a crazy world and gold fever only adds to the madness. The stories we hear of conflict gold from the Democratic Republic of the Congo are true; however, they are only one half of the story. The other half is the one I am here to explore with the UK not-for-profit Peace Direct[2] partners, CRC.

The central conundrum that CRC have identified and want to tackle is, "Can responsible and well-organized small-scale gold mining by ex-combatants lead to genuine peaceful and sustainable transformation?" I had witnessed elements of this idea in my work in securing traceable gold from Colombia from the green gold project in my capacity as founder of CRED Jewellery, the benefits of which are plain to see now that the certified Fairtrade gold programme has grown to four certified mining groups in South America.

CRED Jewellery alone has paid over $100,000 in Fairtrade premiums to their certified gold partners Sotrami in Peru since its launch in February 2011. Sotrami, in turn, have invested this money into education in their community as well as the establishing of a food store that supplies at wholesale prices to the wider community. This is the impact that can be made when you get artisanal mining traceable and certified.

The small towns of Iga Barrière and Kobu are where I start my discovery. The road that takes us there snakes north of Bunia, past a new Chinese gold mining concession and eventually to the highly controversial AngloGold Ashanti mine, near Mongbwalu. But I am not here to investigate the predictably secretive and un-transparent member of the World Gold Council and Responsible Jewellery Council. I am here to review and understand the activity of peace building in the war-torn Democratic Republic of the Congo.

CRC have identified that a key to reducing or deflating the conflict is finding employment for the ex-combatants that inhabit every town and village across the eastern DRC. I admire their boldness as they have chosen to take a proactive stance toward the issue of conflict minerals. I confess, as a veteran campaigner in the jewellery profession for more ethical and fair trade practices, I have arrived with a certain level of unspoken scepticism, but with an open mind to their idea.

It is hard to describe to someone who has never stood in the artisanal gold fields of Africa what the experience is like. To say it is chaotic is to understate the reality of its cousin, horror. It is like stepping into the circle of hell that Dante forgot to write about. Small-scale mining is the second biggest employer on the planet, with a global workforce and dependency in excess of 100 million. They, like Dante's omission, are forgotten; the forgotten millions who for the politics of daily bread pound their bodies in the scorching heat in search of the madness that is gold.

In Iga Barrière, on one level everyone is a millionaire and the vast riches of the gold deposits are a living testimony to the resource curse. One story I hear and verify is that in a one-month period the local miners worked with a Korean called "Mr Dave". And they produced 40 kilos of gold using Dave's mechanized processing unit. Dave, of course, disappeared back to Korea with the 40 kilos without paying, leaving behind a group of defrauded miners and his processing machine. The affected miners show me the site of Dave's machine, now lying on its side in the middle of the fast-flowing Nizi River; a small vignette of how opportunities dissipate through the locals' fingertips like water through a sieve.

The first thing you notice about any small-scale mine site is the constant white noise of the mechanized humming of water pumps and generators. It is a universal sound associated with artisanal and small-scale mining, but it is soon drowned out by the endless chatter of the countless workers, as they dig and haul pans of soil up though the chain gangs to the top of slopes where the content is panned and washed of its muddy content, leaving only fine sands and alluvial gold particles.

All this is backbreaking, dirty, noisy, insecure, and dangerous work carried out on the promise of payment plus a daily meal till the gold is delivered. It is mind-boggling how the sheer muscle of humanity, driven on by the primeval urge to survive, can move tonnes of earth every hour and in doing so carve vast ravines out of hillsides, redirect river courses, and sculpt entirely new landscapes as they pursue the gold veins wherever they may lead.

But to truly understand the ASM sector you need to look beneath the obvious of environmental mismanagement, systemic mercury usage, and the child labour issues and understand the hidden driver of money and survival.

During my journey I talk to a lot of miners in the towns and on the mine sites I visit, and to the traders I encounter. They all tell the same basic story, best illustrated by this one miner in Kobu.

He borrows money from a local trader that will allow him to open up a small pit, which requires that he employs a group of local diggers, maybe as many as forty. These diggers will move the soil until they hit the gold-bearing rock or start to wash the gold from the river sands. If he is digging rock, he will also be loaned some mercury that he will use to amalgam the gold from the rock dust. Mercury and gold particles really do like each other. Once he has extracted his gold, he will have to pay back the trader in gold plus the interest he owes, which can be as much as 30 per cent to 50 per cent. He is then obliged by the terms of the original loan to sell the remaining gold to the same trader at discounted rates on the international gold price. This price is determined by weight and purity of gold sold.

The trader will determine purity through a process called "acid burning", where the gold is heated and melted to molten liquid and burned with acid to remove any material that is not gold. After selling the remaining gold, the miner then pays the government mining group Kilomoto 30 per cent of his income as they have licensed him to work on their concession in the first place. He then pays his workers for their sweat and muscle.

Throughout the time that he opens the pit to the time he finally closes the deal on the gold sale, he has to manage a myriad of different quasi-official interests that are taken in any new mine site. He makes payments to the police, the Congolese security service, soldiers, local government office, local chiefs, and the environmental office, as well as paying the hydro carbon tax (he actually offsets his carbon omissions) and anyone else who may have the power to stop him from mining. If he and his six partners are left with as much as $3,000 between them from a $50,000 transaction for 1 kilo of gold, he will feel himself fortunate. When you ask him why he does it, he simply replies, "It is all I know how to do, and I earn just enough per month to feed my family."

In this region of Ituri I am talking directly to small-scale gold miners who are ex-combatants, who want to use gold mining as a means of building peace, not punishment. Their idea cannot be any worse than the top-down proscriptive process the Organisation for Economic Co-operation and Development (OECD) has recently run in the region regarding conflict minerals. From the very beginning of the OECD process, I could never understand how their rules for governing the export of designated conflict minerals (tin, tantalum, tungsten, and gold), which they refer to as "due diligences in supply chain management", were going to lead to a reduction in the use of gold as a conflict mineral. Ostensibly it is because their process does not address the root causes of what according to CRC is an ethnic conflict in which gold can easily be used to fund the violence.

As if to prove this point, Henri tells me that the previous evening he received a call from a local militia leader in the bush who had ten children with two guns that he wanted to demobilize and rehabilitate back to their families. Why this sudden act of clemency had taken place I never learn, but this is typical of the kind of work that Henri and CRC undertake all the time.

Henri explains that the children will be placed with specially trained families for the first few months, while their families are contacted, and prepared for their return to village life. Their weapons are then decommissioned at the United Nations HQ in Bunia. To take the guns to the Congolese army would mean they would just be recycled back into the conflict, as many soldiers sell the guns to get extra cash. Henri is very clear: children end up in the militia because they and their families are poor. Therefore they make easy targets for militia leaders looking for new recruits for a simple US dollar payment to the family.

None of the miners have ever heard of the OECD or transparency or supply chain management. Nor do they have the ability to read a complex OECD report written by university graduates. All they know is that they currently sell their gold to traders and its destination is Bunia.

The OECD conflict gold process is a politically correct tragedy unfolding before us. If, through a sense of moral outrage at the appalling conflict that has to date claimed 5.5 million lives, we remove the population's ability to earn a living in an honest fashion, then these same people are forced by necessity into militia activity or illegal smuggling to earn a daily crust. As another mining leader in North Kivu once wrote to me to say in response to the Enough Project's[3] call to boycott eastern DRC minerals, "We will die by the bullet or die of starvation." The OECD conflict minerals process deals with the fruit, not the root, of the problem. It is the sticking plaster on the wound, sold to the market as a cure. The root of the problem is poverty. The OECD has created a set of recommended procedures that only corporate mining companies can afford to follow, rather than addressing the majority employed by the gold trade, the small-scale miners and their poor communities.

It is little wonder, then, that the vast mineral wealth of the DRC will not benefit the DRC people through this process. A United Nations Security Council report dated 21 June 2012 highlighted that since the introduction of the measures by the OECD to stem the flow of conflict metals being smuggled into the global supply chain, "The eastern DRC official export figures seem to have been falling rather than increasing." Clearly, however well-intentioned the OECD due diligences on conflict minerals may be, at this stage smuggling is on the increase, which in turn will only lead to more insecurity and violence.

It is not the idea of conflict-free gold that is the problem. Everyone wants an end to the deadly conflict, none more so than the exploited miners. It is the way that corporately influenced OECD top-down guidelines have framed the solution that seems to be adding to the already highly complex problem, rather than making it better. The same security council report talks about the estimated 3 tonnes of gold sold to the international market in 2010 illicitly.

Uganda is the principal destination for this gold, and it ends up in the Dubai refineries, and eventually goes on to India and China. China is the world's biggest jewellery manufacturer with several of the UK's leading high street jewellery brands producing their collections there. There is no doubt in my mind, given the lack of enforceable traceability in the gold supply chain, that smuggled gold that currently funds conflicts is making its way onto the high streets of the UK, EU, and USA in the form of gold jewellery.

It remains to be seen if the OECD due diligences on conflict minerals will work, but what is clear at the moment is they have given the World Gold Council, the London Bullion Market Association (LBMA), and the Responsible Jewellery Council's corporate members another CSR badge to add to their collection.

The sufferings of Job that have been meted out on the people and land of the DRC remains a festering wound on the conscious of humanity. But as Job rightly said, "The light... is near to the darkness," and it is this light of hope, burning brightly in the aspirations of the people I have met on my trip, that gives me such huge encouragement. These are people such as Henri of CRC and the Hima and Lendu ex-combatants, who were historically at war with each other and who now have agreed to form a new association of responsible small-scale miners for peace and justice, and who demonstrate that despite the huge obstacles they will face, they are not burdened down with cynicism about their future. They are like the countless nameless and faceless majority in the DRC who want nothing more than peace and non-violence to triumph in their country.

But this is the DRC, and the metaphorical mountain that this fledgling association of small miners must climb will be bigger than the literal mountain that their large-scale mining cousins blow up and crush to satisfy the greed of the so-called moral stock markets and bank vaults.

I for one will follow with great interest as they attempt to build their future using gold as the means to build peace, not conflict.

GLOSSARY

artisanal mining: small-scale, independent mining using low technology.

assay master: the officer who assays or tests the amounts of gold/silver used in coins, jewellery, or bullion products.

Bajracharya: both a surname and a description of an artisan clan of silversmiths.

batch casting: casting small batches of gold to the required shape in an isolated way, so the metals are not mixed or diluted in any way.

bourse: a stock market or trading floor were rough diamonds are traded.

blood diamonds: the name by which the rough diamonds whose mining, smuggling, and selling funded wars and rebel insurgencies in several African nations became known as.

FLO-CERT: independent auditors and certification body that works with Fairtrade International.

gem quality: the quality or grade of rough gemstones that are able to be cut and polished into a gemstone of good quality for jewellery.

gold fix: the daily price fixing levels for gold that determine the international price.

marquise cut: a specific cut of a diamond or gemstone that looks like an elongated diamond shape.

mass balancing: in gold, the process where the mass going into a system is counted and the same quantity taken out. However, the physical source of the product may be completely different. So a jeweller may buy gold on the open market from a bank, but because their manufacturing is in China, they take out the same amount of gold for their production. The traceability of the gold is not required.

Oro Verdé: a programme established in 2000 to support small-scale mining in the Chocó region of Colombia.

tailings piles: piles of materials left over from separating the valuable from the valueless material during the mining process.

END NOTE TO CONSUMERS

How to purchase ethically sourced jewellery

Beautiful design and a fair price are important considerations for most people shopping for jewellery. But these days, given that the sourcing of jewellery is linked to wars, child labour, and environmental degradation, another question for many concerned about the future is: How can I purchase ethically made jewellery?

Fortunately, this is not so difficult. You can make a huge difference for small-scale producers, artisans, and the environment simply by supporting jewellers who share your values. Plus, even though a piece of jewellery is responsibly sourced, it may still be competitively priced with comparable product. Aligning your economic power with your ethical values just requires that you know the right questions to ask.

The most critical issue in the purchase of ethical jewellery is that it is traceably and transparently sourced, from mine to market. Essentially, you have to know where the material comes from and how it was transformed from rough material mined from the earth to an elegant piece of jewellery behind a glass case. Jewellery is made up of metal, findings, and possibly gemstones. Ask your retailer to specifically tell you where the material comes from back to its source. If possible, have them include where the gem was mined, where it was cut, where the metal came from, and who made the piece.

The response of the salesperson to this question will reveal a lot. When listening, you will get a sense of the ethos of the company. For example, if you ask a salesperson about a diamond and the best they can do is to tell you that it is Kimberley certified conflict-free, that is not a satisfactory answer. Diamonds produced in horrendous conditions can still be labelled "conflict-free". Even if the salesperson tells you the diamond is from Israel or Antwerp, that is not good enough. Those are not diamond-producing countries. Remember, you have to be able to trace product from mine to market. One proper example of an answer would be: "This diamond is mined at the Ekati mine in Canada, and cut in Canada as well." Another example: If you are enquiring about a sapphire, a jeweller may say, "It is from Africa." Not good enough. A good answer would be that the sapphire comes from a cooperative of small-scale miners in Ratnapura, Sri Lanka.

Two other issues are important. First, determine where and how the piece of jewellery was made. Support your neighbourhood jewellery designer, if possible – it's good for your local economy. Secondly, ask where the metal in the jewellery comes from. These days, every piece of non-Fairtrade jewellery you buy should at least be made with 100 per cent recycled metals. It should not cost you more and it does help the environment a little bit. But the problem with recycled metals is that no matter how much is used, precious metal will still be mined. So by purchasing jewellery made from certified Fairtrade gold or silver you are directly supporting responsible small-scale mining communities. It is truly the most precious of all metal processes in the world.

In summary, there are only a few things you need to consider: where the metal comes from, where the gem comes from, and how the jewellery is made? These days, only a rare jeweller will be able to answer all these questions. The supply chains for jewellery are very much still in the early phases of development. Many jewellers sell product that is partially ethical – just as there are food markets that offer a good selection of organics but are not totally organic. Support these pioneer ethical jewellery companies, too. We want to build a broad market and those jewellers who are offering even smaller collections of responsibly sourced product are worthy of support. If just 5 per cent of people walking into jewellery stores asked for ethical product, the demand would have a huge impact around the world.

Buying jewellery is a wonderful opportunity for everyone to celebrate special moments in the lives of those they love. Make sure the jewellery you buy also celebrates the lives of those who mined it and made it as well.

For more information on ethical sources of jewellery, please visit the Fair Jewelry Action website, www.fairjewelry.org.

Marc Choyt
Co-founder of Fair Jewelry Action and Owner of Reflective Images, Santa Fe, New Mexico

NOTES

Chapter One

1. B. Jackson, *Poverty and the Planet: A Question of Survival*, London: Penguin, 1990.

E. F. Schumacher, *Small is Beautiful: A Study of Economics as if People Mattered*, London: Vintage Books, 1973.

P. Vallely, *Bad Samaritans: First World Ethics and Third World Debt*, New York: Orbis Books, 1990.

J. H. Yoder, *The Politics of Jesus*, Grand Rapids, MI: Eerdmans, 1972.

2. Structural Adjustment refers to a set of economic policies often introduced as a condition for gaining a loan from the IMF. Structural adjustment policies usually involve a combination of free market policies such as privatization, fiscal austerity, free trade, and deregulation. Structural adjustment policies have been controversial, with detractors arguing the free market policies are often unsuitable for developing economies and lead to lower economic growth and greater inequality. Supporters of structural adjustment (IMF and World Bank) argue that these free market reforms are essential for promoting a more open and efficient economy. For more information I recommend the following website: http://www.economicshelp.org/dictionary/s/ structural-adjustment.html (accessed 3 June 2013).

Chapter Two

1. Meron and Sarai's story is the subject of another book I may write one day. I stayed in touch with them both throughout the nineties. In fact, I was sitting in their shared slum house having coffee when I heard of the death of Princess Diana.

2. See the Gospel of Matthew 25:40.

Chapter Three

1. S. Wal, *Child Labour in Various Industries* Vol. 3, New Delhi: Sarup & Sons, 2006, p. 285.

2. Dante, *The First Three Circles of Hell* (D. L. Sayers, ed.; D. L. Sayers, trans.) London: Penguin, 1949, p. 21.

Chapter Five
1. Isaiah 45:3.

Chapter Seven
1. http://www.communitymining.org/index.php/en/about-us (accessed 6 June 2013).

2. http://www.anglogold.com/Additional/Press/2007/Geita+Gold+Mine+experiences+partial+slope+failure+in+Nyankanga+pit.htm (accessed 6 June 2013).

3. http://reliefweb.int/report/hungary/baia-mare-gold-mine-cyanide-spill-causes-impacts-and-liability (accessed 6 June 2013).

4. http://www.earthworksaction.org/voices/detail/cajamarca#.ULTkE4W-2qY (accessed 6 June 2013).

Chapter Nine
1. See http://news.bbc.co.uk/1/hi/world/europe/8111292.stm (accessed 7 June 2013).

2. See Inuit Circumpolar Council, Principles and Elements for a Comprehensive Arctic Policy, Montreal: Centre for Northern Studies and Research, McGill University, 1992, pp. 48–51.

Chapter Ten
1. http://www.cyanidecode.org/about-code/cyanide-code (accessed 7 June 2013).

2. http://www.fairjewelry.org/?p=2205 (accessed 11 June 2013).

Chapter Eleven
1. "Uplifting the Earth" is available to download from http://www.fairjewelry.org/resources/key-reports-documents/reports-on-jewelry-in-general/ (accessed 11 June 2013).

2. Lifeworth are a network of independent researchers and educators who focus their time and energy on promoting sustainability and social and environmental development. See www.lifeworth.com

Epilogue

1. Job 17:12.

2. Peace Direct is a London-based charity that supports peace builders in conflict areas.

3. The Enough Project is based in Washington DC, and campaigns to end genocide and crimes against humanity.